Cambridge Elements ☰

Elements in Business Strategy
edited by
J.-C. Spender
Kozminski University

THE CREATIVE RESPONSE

Knowledge and Innovation

Cristiano Antonelli
University of Turin

Alessandra Colombelli
Politecnico di Torino

CAMBRIDGE
UNIVERSITY PRESS

Shaftesbury Road, Cambridge CB2 8EA, United Kingdom

One Liberty Plaza, 20th Floor, New York, NY 10006, USA

477 Williamstown Road, Port Melbourne, VIC 3207, Australia

314–321, 3rd Floor, Plot 3, Splendor Forum, Jasola District Centre, New Delhi – 110025, India

103 Penang Road, #05–06/07, Visioncrest Commercial, Singapore 238467

Cambridge University Press is part of Cambridge University Press & Assessment, a department of the University of Cambridge.

We share the University's mission to contribute to society through the pursuit of education, learning and research at the highest international levels of excellence.

www.cambridge.org
Information on this title: www.cambridge.org/9781108987424

DOI: 10.1017/9781108987547

First published 2023

A catalogue record for this publication is available from the British Library.

ISBN 978-1-108-98742-4 Paperback
ISSN 2515-0693 (online)
ISSN 2515-0685 (print)

The Creative Response

Knowledge and Innovation

Elements in Business Strategy

DOI: 10.1017/9781108987547
First published online: February 2023

Cristiano Antonelli
University of Turin

Alessandra Colombelli
Politecnico di Torino

Author for correspondence: Cristiano Antonelli, cristiano.antonelli@unito.it

Abstract: This Element combines the advances of the economics of knowledge and innovation implementing the Schumpeterian notion of creative response to understand the determinants and the effects of the rate and direction of technological and organizational change and its variance across time and space, firms, and industries. The notion of creative response provides an inclusive framework that enables us to highlight the crucial role of knowledge in assessing the rate and direction of technological change and to clarify that no innovation is possible without the generation of new knowledge, while the generation of new knowledge augments the chances of innovation but does not automatically yield the introduction of innovation. Firms thus are faced with several strategic decisions to make the creative response possible. The Element elaborates on the analytical core of the notion of creative response and articulates its implications for economic policy and strategic management.

Keywords: creative response, innovation function, knowledge generation function, technology production function, technological change

ISBNs: 9781108987424 (PB), 9781108987547 (OC)
ISSNs: 2515-0693 (online), 2515-0685 (print)

Contents

1 Introduction

Innovation is an emergent system property that may take place when the entrepreneurial response to unexpected factor and product market conditions is complemented and supported by conducive systemic conditions that enable the generation of indispensable technological knowledge at costs below equilibrium. This Element uses the tools of evolutionary complexity building upon the notion of creative response introduced by Joseph Schumpeter in "The creative response in economic history." The Element provides the foundations of an inclusive framework that enables us to integrate the variety of mechanisms considered by the different streams of literature to grasp the dynamics of the endogenous innovation process and to identify the crucial role of knowledge in assessing the rate and the direction of technological change and their effects in terms of productivity, profitability, and growth.

The contribution of Schumpeter published by the *Journal of Economic History* in 1947 can be regarded as the synthesis of his lifelong research on the role of innovation in economics. "The creative response in economic history" synthesizes in a unified framework the ingredients elaborated in "The instability of capitalism," published by the *Economic Journal* (Schumpeter, 1928); *The Theory of Economic Development*, published in English in 1934 (Schumpeter, 1911–1934); *Business Cycles: A Theoretical, Historical and Statistical Analysis of the Capitalist Process* (Schumpeter, 1939); and *Capitalism, Socialism and Democracy* (Schumpeter, 1942). It combines the basic tools of textbook microeconomics – such as analysis of technical change as a reactive movement on the existing map of isoquants in response to changes in product and factor markets – and key Marshallian contributions – such as the role of variety and of externalities – with analysis of the intentional introduction of innovations as a creative response that is able to change the existing map of isoquants when the systemic conditions into which firms are embedded support their entrepreneurial action (Antonelli, 2017b, 2018c). This framework enables appreciation of the central role of intentional decision-making in the generation of technological knowledge and the introduction of innovations as a response to the challenges and opportunities provided by changing product and factor market conditions and access to the general stock of scientific and technological knowledge.

The framework of the creative response seems especially appropriate for analyzing the evolutionary complexity of endogenous innovation and variety based upon the dynamics of feedback between individual decision-making and systemic changes that characterize the working of economics systems and especially of the global economy where firms, based in local factor markets with resilient diversities, compete in quasi-homogenous international product markets. Globalization has become the engine of the creative response that enables advanced economies to cope with the rapid and radical changing of product and factor markets by means of the introduction of innovations with high levels of knowledge intensity, an input that is relatively abundant in advanced economies and quite rare in industrializing countries.

Section 2 presents a sequential system of equations (SSE) to enable analysis of the determinants of endogenous introduction of innovations by firms exposed to unexpected changes in their product and factor markets, as a creative response that is strictly contingent upon the size and composition of the stock of existing knowledge, as well as its access and use conditions, which feed the recombinant generation of new knowledge. The SSE includes in the first step the amount of innovative effort of each firm, which is contingent upon the changing conditions of product and factor markets. Firms are reluctant to undertake risky activities characterized by high levels of unpredictability and uncertainty; this risk-averseness and their commitment to innovate are intentional as stirred by specific and idiosyncratic constraints and opportunities that need to be identified and assessed. Firms purposely undertake risky innovative activities only when they have clear incentives and opportunities.

As the second equation of the SSE shows, the outcome of their innovation effort depends upon the amount, quality, and variety of the stock of technological knowledge, both internal and external to each firm, that can be used to generate new technological knowledge that is indispensable to the introduction of innovations. The conditions for accessing such stock(s) are crucial in identifying the actual amount of technological knowledge that each firm can generate. The third equation analyzes the introduction of the amount of knowledge generated into the technology production function. The final equations show that the rate and the direction of technological change are emergent system properties that are the outcome of the concurrent and complementary role of entrepreneurial action and of the systemic characteristics of its context of action.

The following sections explore in detail each equation of the SSE. Section 3 explores the innovation function according to which the introduction of innovation may take place when firms caught in out-of-equilibrium conditions try to elaborate a response. Entry of new competitors, changes in aggregate demand, changes in consumer preferences, competitors' introduction of innovations, and changes in input costs are all continual sources of surprise for firms. Decision-making is characterized by bounded rather than Olympian rationality. The mismatch between expected and actual product and factor market conditions engenders a reaction based upon procedural rationality. Such a reaction can be creative and consists in the introduction of innovations when firms can generate the necessary amount of technological knowledge at costs that are below equilibrium because they can access and use the full stock of existing knowledge and recombine it with their internal knowledge stock. When firms do not have access to technological knowledge stocks and cannot benefit from relevant pecuniary knowledge externalities, the response is just adaptive and its outcome consists of novelties rather than productivity-and-profitability-enhancing innovations.

Section 4 explores the mechanisms of the recombinant generation of new technological knowledge. Top-down and bottom-up processes of knowledge generation complement each other within the borders of the firm: learning and formalized research activities are strictly complementary, as much as internal and external knowledge. The richer the stock of knowledge in terms of both size and variety, the better the access and use conditions in the recombination and the larger the output in terms of new knowledge. The limited appropriability and exhaustibility of knowledge feed the accumulation of stocks of quasi-public knowledge. Access to and use of the stock of existing knowledge, however, is far from free: it entails dedicated activities to screen, identify, decode, learn, and finally use it. Transferability of knowledge is actually limited. Knowledge is necessarily embodied in human beings. Personal interactions are indispensable in order to use knowledge because of its intrinsically tacit content. Geographical, institutional, professional, cognitive, and technological proximity helps in accessing existing knowledge. Being able to identify, appreciate, and accurately select the procedures and mechanisms that enable access to and use of external stocks of quasi-public knowledge becomes a crucial factor of both economic analysis and strategic management. Next to imitating competitors are all the absorption mechanisms of the other, different sources of external knowledge such as upstream and downstream user–producer relations, public research centers, and a mobile talent pool.

Section 5 explores the role of endogenous knowledge in the production of all other goods. In the technology production function implemented by this Element, the stock of knowledge has been decided in an upstream decision process: as such, it enters the technology production function as a fixed factor. The capitalization of knowledge marks a central step in the twin evolution of the economics of innovation and knowledge. Capitalized knowledge itself is at the same time an input in the technology production function and the output of the upstream knowledge generation function.

Section 6 shows how the strategic direction of technological change toward the intensive use of exclusive inputs, such as technological knowledge, that are locally abundant but not accessible, at the same conditions, by rivals in international product markets can help firms increase the appropriability of both the technological knowledge generated and the innovations introduced. Rivals that cannot use the very same factor markets can imitate but cannot (re)produce at the same costs. The increasing role of technological knowledge and human capital as essential and indispensable production factors and at the same time key outputs of advanced economies is the direct consequence of the creative response of firms that are more and more engaged in direct rivalry with firms based in labor-abundant but knowledge-scarce economies. Globalization is the key driver toward a knowledge economy. Firms based in advanced economies have a strong incentive to accelerate the introduction of innovations and to bias technological change toward knowledge-intensive directions for two deeply intertwined reasons: both knowledge and human capital are becoming cheaper and cheaper with respect to other inputs in the local factor markets of advanced economies and much cheaper than in the factor markets of competing firms based in industrializing countries.

Section 7 shows how and why the outcome of the response to the out-of-equilibrium changes of product and factor markets yields changes to production processes, products, organizations, markets, and input mixes that account for the improved performance, that is, the actual increase of total factor productivity (TFP) and profitability, only if, when, and where the pervasive effects of the limited appropriability and exhaustibility of technological knowledge trigger access to and use of the existing knowledge stock and its use to generate new knowledge at costs below equilibrium. When the conditions of access to the general knowledge stock are not able to support the recombinant generation of technological knowledge, the response is adaptive: firms can introduce only novelties that are not able to yield any increase in productivity and profitability.

Finally, Section 8 summarizes the analysis of Schumpeterian loops triggered by the creative framework and stresses its dynamic implications. The response of firms to emerging out-of-equilibrium conditions of product and factor markets enhanced by the rapid globalization of the economy, when and if supported by access to localized technological knowledge stocks, accounts for the endogenous introduction of technological changes and the endogenous reproduction of variety in product and factor markets.

Such technological changes, moreover, in turn trigger new waves of changes not only in product and factor markets but also in the size and composition of the knowledge stock – via the accumulation of new vintages of knowledge that add to the existing stocks because of the limited exhaustibility of knowledge that is affected by actual obsolescence and wear and tear only to a limited extent – and in the systems of knowledge interactions that make possible the access to and use of the stocks of technological knowledge at costs below equilibrium. The conditions of access to, together with the size and composition of, the quasi-public knowledge stock yield the pecuniary knowledge externalities that enable a creative response and the eventual introduction of productivity-and-profitability-enhancing innovations.

Innovation may emerge as a recursive system property that takes place within path-dependent processes that are non-ergodic, as they are historic processes where time matters, but far from deterministic, as stochastic events may play a major role and original trajectories may be discontinued and altered by small events that take place along the process. Innovation may take place when agents that try to implement their responses to the changing conditions of product and factor markets are able to put in place convergent research strategies that favor the recombinant generation of new technological knowledge within actual coalitions for growth that are able to identify, strengthen, valorize, and exploit latent knowledge complementarities and open the way to Schumpeterian loops of recursive rounds of creative responses that spread in the system.

2 The Framework of the Creative Response

2.1 Introduction

The introduction of innovations requires the preliminary and indispensable generation of specific and dedicated technological knowledge. The introduction of new products, new processes, new organizational models and procedures, input mixes, and entry into new markets requires the use of dedicated technological knowledge. Both the generation of technological knowledge and the introduction of innovations are the outcome of an intentional and dedicated sequence of activities. Firms make conscious decisions to introduce new technologies; technological changes do not simply fall from heaven, just as innovations are not introduced by chance at random. The introduction of innovations is not automatic; it is the outcome of an array of sequential choices and decisions that are characterized by high levels of risk close to uncertainty and take place only in a specific context (Antonelli, 2022b).

The generation of technological knowledge is affected by high levels of risk about the outcome and the appropriability of the output. The Arrovian analysis of knowledge as an economic good highlighted the limited appropriability of knowledge, its low levels of excludability and consequently the low levels of fundability and tradability (Arrow, 1962a, 1969). According to the Arrovian synthesis of the Schumpeterian analysis of the short duration of transient monopolistic rents due to the imitative entry of rivals, "inventors" can retain only a limited fraction of the full stream of benefits triggered by the introduction of innovations.

The limited appropriability of the economic returns stemming from the generation of technical knowledge, however, comes second after their substantial unpredictability. The timing and content of the output of the activities, ranging from formal research and development (R&D) to learning procedures and competence-implementing procedures, finalized to generate new knowledge must consider the high levels of uncertainty about the actual outcome of the generation process. The knowledge generation process may lead to unexpected results with contents that are far from the expected ones: a trip directed to the south-east of the knowledge map may easily end up in the north-west. The distance that the research unit is able to reach may be quite small, far below the expected levels. The matching between the resources invested and the results obtained is often quite poor, far below that in any other economic activity. Occasionally, if not rarely, the generation of knowledge takes place within planned timing, yields the expected results in terms of scope of application, and produces a stream of economic benefits, from both its generation and its application, that is larger than its costs.

When the generation of technological knowledge yields positive outcomes, the introduction of innovations, in turn, can take place, but in a context of high levels of product and market risks. As Robert Merton points out:

> New products and services are created to enable people to do tasks better than they previously could or do things they couldn't before. But innovations also carry risks. Just how risky an innovation turns out to be depends in great measure on the choices people make in using it. Attempts to gauge the riskiness of an innovation must take into account the limitations of the models – formal and informal – on which people base their decisions about how to use the innovation . . .. Some models turn out to be fundamentally flawed and should be jettisoned . . . while others are merely incomplete and can be improved upon. Some models require sophisticated users to produce good results; others are suitable only to certain applications. And even when people employ appropriate models to make choices about how to use an innovation—striking the right balance between risk and performance— experience shows that it is almost impossible to predict how their changed behavior will influence the riskiness of other choices and behaviors they make, often in apparently unrelated domains. It's the old story of unintended consequences. The more complex the system an innovation enters, the more likely and severe its unintended consequences will be. Indeed, many of the risks associated with an innovation stem not from the innovation itself but from the infrastructure into which it is introduced. In the end, any innovation involves a leap into the unknowable. If we are to make progress, however, that's a fact we need to accept and to manage. (Merton, 2013, p. 1)

The risks intrinsic to the generation of new technological knowledge add to the risks of attempting to introduce an innovation that enables actual increase in profitability and productivity. Their sequential combination yields conditions of uncertainty. Firms are reluctant to take these risks and their capability to handle such high levels of uncertainty is limited. The intentional decision to generate new technological knowledge and to innovate is implemented only when the specific out-of-equilibrium conditions of product and factor markets impede business as usual and solicit dedicated efforts to cope with the unexpected conditions by means of the generation of new technological knowledge and the introduction of innovations.

The decision to undertake the substantial risks of innovation activities that characterize both the upstream generation and the downstream use of new technological knowledge to introduce and exploit an innovation is not an automatic process. It takes place only in a specific economic context characterized by challenges that impede firms' ability to conduct business as usual and provide rare opportunities. In equilibrium, when the evolution of product and factor markets matches standard expectations, firms are not ready to take such risks. Here the prospect theory, according to which firms are more sensitive to losses than gains and strongly tend to avoid losses, helps us to grasp the determinants of decision-making about innovative efforts (Tversky and Kahneman, 1992).

The economics of knowledge and innovation have little investigated the context in which decision-making about the generation of technological knowledge and the introduction of innovations takes place: the leading approaches – standard evolutionary approaches and the new growth theory – do not explore the determinants of innovative efforts as an intentional process. Standard evolutionary approaches of Darwinist ascent assume that firms keep innovating at all times and that generation of knowledge is based on automatic learning processes that are implemented by routines (Nelson and Winter, 1982). This literature assumes that firms decide levels of R&D expenditure following automatic rules of thumb such as fixed fractions of past sales. Evolutionary approaches do not take into account the effects on discretionary decision-making of the changing conditions of product and factor markets that lead to the definition of firms' innovative efforts. Standard evolutionary approaches are not able to explain why some firms innovate more than others, or why firms are much more innovative at certain times than at others (Dosi and Nelson, 2010).

The new growth theory also does not elaborate on the determinants of firms' innovation efforts; rather, it centers its analysis on the special properties of technological knowledge as an economic good and values limited appropriability as the engine of increasing returns disseminated by externalities that yield TFP growth at the aggregate and the firm level. In the new growth theory, knowledge that is not fully appropriated by "inventors" spills into the system and benefits third parties that, in turn, can generate new knowledge and introduce innovations. Firms optimize their use of knowledge as an input – characterized by a reduced output elasticity because of its limited appropriability – in a production function – the so-called technology production function enriched by inclusion of knowledge – according to the matching between the costs and the output elasticity of all the inputs. The new growth theory does not take into account the high levels of knowledge generation and exploitation risk that come with the introduction of innovations (Romer, 1990, 1994; Aghion and Howitt, 1997; Aghion and Jaravel, 2015).

More specifically the new growth theory assumes that the limited appropriability of knowledge reflects its high transferability such that knowledge spillovers yield technical externalities that benefit all the agents of the system at all times and in all locations with no costs. The new growth theory does not take into account the possibility that the limited appropriability of knowledge coexists with its limited transferability. The limited transferability of knowledge stems from the costs of screening, assessing, accessing, absorbing, and finally using external knowledge generated by third parties. Only a few firms with high levels of geographical, institutional, cognitive, and technological proximity can take full advantage of the spillover stemming from the limited appropriability of knowledge.

The combination of limited appropriability and limited transferability dramatically curbs the heuristic power of the new growth theory. That only a few firms are able to take advantage of spillovers dramatically limits the incentives to generate new knowledge: in any simple oligopolistic market, it is sufficient that a few firms take advantage of free spillovers sequentially, drawing nil profits from innovation and instead transferring all benefits to consumers. Yet, the vast majority of firms, based at a distance, are not able to take advantage of free spillovers and must bear heavy absorption costs, which dramatically limits any positive effects (Cohen and Levinthal, 1990). Knowledge externalities are pecuniary rather than technical and the limited transferability of knowledge drastically reduces its positive effects for all but a few firms, and consequently for the system at large (Antonelli, 2022a).

This Element takes an evolutionary complexity approach that impinges upon the Schumpeterian framework of the creative response (Schumpeter, 1947). It appreciates the endogenous heterogeneity of agents and credits them with the capability to change their knowledge and technology when and if their context of action stirs and supports their response (Antonelli, 2011, 2017a).

The framework of the creative response provides the foundations upon which to articulate an inclusive evolutionary complexity where growth and change are explained by the coupling of the capability of agents to react to unexpected changes in their product and factor markets and the access to knowledge externalities that is available within the system. Innovation and variety are fully endogenous as they are emerging system properties, although they depend upon highly idiosyncratic characteristics of the system (Foster and Metcalfe, 2012).

The approach taken in this Element enables us to stress the specific intentionality of the introduction of innovations and the context in which it takes place so as to appreciate the Lamarckian contributions to evolutionary economics. We can build the framework of the creative response quite effectively using the recent advances in the economics of knowledge. These enable us to overcome the limitations both of standard evolutionary economics, which are based upon grafting Darwinian legacies according to which variety is generated automatically and not purposely, and of the new growth theory, which builds upon knowledge spillovers but regards innovation as the outcome of standard maximization procedures of decision-making that do not take into account the coexistence of substantial limits to both the appropriability and the transferability of knowledge (Bolton, 1993; Munoz and Encinar, 2014; Erixon, 2016; Manzaneque et al., 2020). This framework of evolutionary complexity based upon the creative response is quite comprehensive as it includes, as drivers of the decision to innovate, not only the classic Schumpeterian oligopolistic rivalry but also the classical dynamics of induced technological change, where changes in cost factors stir the introduction of innovations directed at reducing the intensity of inputs that are – becoming – more expensive, and the demand-pull approach, where increased demand helps expand the division of labor, augmenting the levels of specialization and of creativity (Antonelli, 2017a, 2017b).

In the creative response framework, firms have a limited ability to see into the future and yet need to make long-term decisions that include introducing innovations when the context in which they are embedded triggers – and supports – their innovative efforts (Massenot and Pettinicchi, 2018). When the evolution of their product and factor markets does not meet their expectations, firms, now in out-of-equilibrium conditions and experiencing below or above equilibrium profitability, make intentional efforts to implement a creative response by introducing innovations and generating the necessary new technological knowledge. The response is creative when the generation of the necessary technological knowledge is supported by the conditions of access to the stock of technological knowledge that is available in the context in which the firms' action is embedded, enabling them to take advantage of relevant pecuniary externalities. Firms in equilibrium conditions, achieving average levels of profitability, have little incentive or opportunity to engage in innovative efforts.

The introduction of technological innovations, in turn, triggers new waves of other changes – not only in product and factor markets but also in the size and composition of the stock of quasi-public knowledge embedded in the system and its access conditions, which trigger the levels of pecuniary knowledge externalities and enable the creative response. The dynamics are far from deterministic as they are intrinsically path-dependent and stochastic. The new waves of changes, in fact, may support persistent Schumpeterian loops if they contribute to the coupling of new out-of-equilibrium conditions and new pecuniary knowledge externalities, or if they worsen the conditions of access to the stocks of quasi-public knowledge and thus reduce the levels of pecuniary knowledge externalities, in turn possibly triggering a drive toward static equilibrium where innovation and growth are no longer possible.

Evolutionary complexity based upon the creative response provides the basic tools we need to understand the working of economic systems at large, but its scope of application is widely enhanced and augmented in the global economy where variety and heterogeneity are magnified. In the global economy, the scope of the creative response is empowered by the interactions in quasi-homogenous international product markets of agents based in highly heterogeneous factor markets shaped by the strong resilience of their idiosyncratic characteristics.

The framework of the creative response also helps us grasp the dynamics of technological change stirred by advanced economies increasingly being exposed to global markets. The rapid pace of globalization since the end of the last century has deeply affected both the product and the factor markets of the world economy and triggered radical changes in the international division of labor and in the specialization of trading partners with recurrent out-of-equilibrium conditions. Engagement in international product markets exposes firms to continual challenges and opportunities because of the relevant knowledge spilling over from more advanced rivals; consequently, it raises the scope for creative responses that increase levels of productivity. In turn, firms with high levels of productivity experience further good performance in international product markets.

2.2 The Evolutionary Complexity of the Creative Response

Reappraising the Schumpeterian notion of creative response enables us to take into account the specific and highly idiosyncratic conditions that explain why, how, and when firms actually decide to bear the high levels of risk associated with generating new technological knowledge and become able to introduce innovations. In the creative response framework, the context in which firms are embedded plays a central role on two counts. First, the conditions of product and factor markets are central to explaining why firms innovate and become ready to bear the high risks. Second, how much knowledge spillover is available and how much it can contribute to individual firms' knowledge generation process depends upon the specific and, once more, highly idiosyncratic conditions in which those firms are embedded in terms of the quality of the knowledge governance mechanism at work in each specific context of action. Let us analyze them in turn.

2.2.1 Conditions of Product and Factor Markets

In the creative response framework, innovation is a high-risk activity, and its outcome is strongly affected by the context in which it takes place. Firms are risk-averse, and their innovative efforts are decided only when product and factor markets are out of equilibrium. Firms try to cope with the new risky context by intentionally performing risky innovation activities that may lead to the eventual introduction of innovations, but only in specific and quite idiosyncratic circumstances. The creative response framework elaborates and impinges upon a strong Lamarckian trait: that change in behavior and introduction of innovations depend upon changes in the context of action. Firms innovate only if specific opportunities and constraints undermine their conducting of business as usual and stir their attempts to change. The Lamarckian hypothesis that the phenotype could change the genotype such that new conducts and behaviors could be transmitted through generation was falsified in biology and genetics, but it applies effectively to the economic analysis of innovation and knowledge. It also contributes to implementing a more comprehensive and inclusive evolutionary economics where endogenous variety and innovation are emergent properties of the system that not only support each other but may be able to contrast both the intrinsic thrusts of competitive markets toward equilibrium and the powerful effects of Darwinian selection on firms that perform less well with the eventual reduction of variety to homogeneity. Firms try to innovate when the actual and unexpected conditions of the product and factor markets in which they operate either (i) undermine their performance such that it falls to below-average levels of sustainability; or (ii) yield above-average performance and provide internal resources that can be invested in risky undertakings. Let us elaborate on this approach briefly.

The actual effects of innovative efforts in terms of performance and TFP growth are determined by the actual cost of technological knowledge. The actual user cost of technological knowledge is determined by two contrasting forces: its limited appropriability and exhaustibility, which make possible low-cost access to existing knowledge generated by third parties – albeit to only a few firms – and the screening and absorption costs that add on and may push the actual user cost close to the equilibrium costs dictated by its reproduction costs.

The attempt to generate new technological knowledge and introduce productivity-enhancing innovations is successful only if, where, and when the conditions of the economic system rooted in the architecture of interactions and transactions are conducive to enabling firms to identify, access, absorb, and use the stock of quasi-public technological knowledge at costs below equilibrium levels.

The large literature that impinges upon the new growth theory assumes that knowledge spills freely into the atmosphere and can be accessed and used by any number of third parties at no cost. The new growth theory has found a new manna: the limited appropriability of knowledge reduces incentives to undertake innovative efforts but also automatically helps reduce the cost of knowledge with technical knowledge externalities to all agents in the system at the same conditions. External knowledge enters the production function of all firms as an unpaid factor and yields the typical technical externalities (Scitovsky, 1954).

This approach is contrasted by investigations into the economics of knowledge that have identified and appreciated the key role both of the limited transferability of knowledge and of knowledge absorption costs. Access to and use of knowledge spillovers require dedicated and expensive activities (Mansfield et al., 1981; Cohen and Levinthal, 1990). The response of firms in out-of-equilibrium conditions is creative and enables the introduction of productivity-enhancing innovations only when pecuniary knowledge externalities reduce the cost of knowledge as an indispensable input in the recombinant generation of new technological knowledge, below the equilibrium level, that is, the cost of reproduction.

Changes in products, processes, input mixes, organizations, and markets are innovations only if they trigger an increase in TFP. Changes are innovations only if they enhance productivity levels. As such, innovations are an emergent property of the system in an endogenous loop where: (i) the system engenders the out-of-equilibrium conditions of product and factor markets; (ii) it enables firms to introduce innovations only if, when, and where it provides them with the opportunity to generate new technological knowledge at costs below equilibrium; (iii) both the out-of-equilibrium conditions and the levels of pecuniary knowledge externalities are endogenous as they are shaped by the decisions to try to innovate and to generate new – additional – technological knowledge; and (iv) the limited appropriability of knowledge means that firms are better off imitating already successful innovations, thus making use of market-sorting mechanisms.

Firms' reactivity levels, the size and composition of the quasi-public technological knowledge stock, and the quality of the knowledge governance mechanism that controls who can access and use that knowledge stock may accelerate or slow down the endogenous dynamics of the creative response. Firms whose innovative efforts are not complemented by systemic conditions and knowledge governance mechanisms that enable them to take advantage of the stock of quasi-public knowledge to generate new technological knowledge at costs below equilibrium – reproduction – levels end up producing just novelties, rather than productivity-enhancing innovations (Akcigit and Liu, 2016).

Levels of innovation effort are defined by the extent of the changes in the product and factor markets with respect to the necessary expectations upon which firms base their decisions. The stronger the dynamics of the product and factor markets, the larger the variance of prices, quantities, and performances and the larger the efforts to try to change the current conduct of business levels by introducing changes. The support of pecuniary knowledge externalities will qualify the extent to which such changes are innovative, that is, the extent to which the response is actually creative or just adaptive.

In the latter case, the changes are not able to reduce costs; the innovation efforts fail to produce anything substantial. In the former case, the specific access to and use of both the quasi-public knowledge stock and the consequent pecuniary knowledge externalities make the response truly creative, thus enabling the introduction of productivity-and-profitability-enhancing innovations.

The system is in equilibrium when the total cost of innovation efforts equals the output of technological knowledge. In this case, the outcome of the innovation efforts consists of novelties. As seen before, novelties differ from innovations because they do not augment the firm's productivity.

2.2.2 Knowledge Spillovers

Technological knowledge is an economic good with special properties: its limited exhaustibility enables its repeated use upstream and downstream (Antonelli, 2018a, 2018b). Because of the limited appropriability of technological knowledge, existing knowledge becomes eventually quasi-public as it spills from its actual owner and possessor to third parties that can use it and benefit from the difference between its costs of absorption and its costs of reproduction. Technological knowledge is, at the same time, the output of the dedicated activities implemented upstream to generate it and an input: existing knowledge is necessary to generate new knowledge. Moreover, technological knowledge is an input into the downstream technology production function of all the other goods.

The limited transferability of knowledge, however, impedes free access to knowledge spilling from third parties. All technological knowledge is characterized by irreducible levels of tacitness: even the most codified piece of knowledge requires considerable learning efforts. Prospective users that cannot take advantage of geographic, knowledge, or institutional proximity experience the limits of knowledge transferability, which may heavily affect the costs of external knowledge. Its effective absorption is helped by user–producer personal interactions. When spillover takes place without the assistance and cooperation of the "producer," absorption costs are higher: in extreme circumstances the costs of absorption may become quite close to the costs of the original generation.

Analysis and appreciation of the limited transferability of knowledge highlight three important aspects: (i) the role of proximity; (ii) the role of absorption costs; and (iii) the role of the composition of the stock of knowledge and its complementarity. Let us analyze them in turn.

(i)   Proximity, in all its facets, matters when it comes to absorbing technological knowledge. Knowledge spills within a limited distance: the effects of spillover decline with distance. The farther the distance between the source and the reception of the spilling knowledge, the lower the opportunity to benefit from its limited appropriability and exclusivity. Interactions are carriers of knowledge spillovers. Interactions in turn take place with stronger intensity within a limited regional space. Next to regional distance, cognitive and technological distance matter: the stronger the sharing of the very same tacit knowledge base, the larger the opportunity that knowledge spillovers will actually take place at low costs (Boschma and Frenken, 2011a, 2011b; Antonelli and David, 2016).

(ii) In relation to absorption costs, understanding them, as well as the notion of user-competence, allows appreciation of the distinction between technical and pecuniary externalities. In Arrovian analysis, spillovers trigger technical externalities that flow in the air and benefit all potential users. If spillover absorption costs are relevant, but lower than invention costs, then pecuniary rather than technical externalities apply and are enjoyed by the spillover recipients. The levels of these pecuniary benefits depend on each agent's endowment of generic competences and learning capabilities, and the specific conditions of the system in which the agents operate (Antonelli, 2008).

(iii) The outcome of the recombinant generation of new technological knowledge depends on the complementarity of the stock of quasi-public technological knowledge embedded in regional, technological, and sectoral systems with the stock of knowledge that is internal to the firm. The complementarity of these external and internal stocks of knowledge plays a central role in the viability of the recombinant process of knowledge generation. Some regions may provide access to specific knowledge items that enable their recombination with the internal stock; others may lack those specific external knowledge inputs.

Proximity exerts strong effects on complementarity. Technological proximity triggers cognitive proximity: industries that belong to the same value chain share tacit knowledge that shapes regional development trajectories. The size and the composition of the stock of competences accumulated over time are likely to create dynamic irreversibility, engendering path-dependent diversification dynamics. In this context, the interplay between regional idiosyncratic features and the ability of local agents to engage in successful learning processes that build upon localized complementarities is considered key to enhancing generation of technological knowledge at costs below equilibrium (Balland et al., 2019; Boschma et al., 2013, Boschma, Heimeriks, and Balland, 2014; Colombelli et al., 2014; Essletzbichler, 2015; Montresor and Quataro, 2017).

Technological knowledge can be regarded not only as an economic good but also as the outcome of an intentional economic activity characterized by high levels of rooting: technological knowledge is intrinsically localized. Knowledge resources are in fact highly idiosyncratic, non-substitutable, resilient, rare, and valuable. Competences emerging out of localized learning are mostly specific to sectors, regions, and technological domains, and therefore hardly useful for activities that are loosely related to existing bundles of regional activity. For this reason, the dynamics of emergence of innovations and new activities are shaped by path-dependence that in turn shapes the direction of technological knowledge. The cost and the composition of new technological knowledge, at each point in time, are heavily affected by the size and the composition of the existing stock of regional knowledge: Jacobs externalities matter as much as Marshallian externalities (Jacobs, 1969; Quataro, 2009; Neffke et al., 2018). The response is all the more creative when the costs of new technological knowledge are below equilibrium levels because the strategic management of research activities is able to: (i) screen items of localized quasi-public knowledge stocks and their specific knowledge spillovers that are at the same time locally abundant and yet exclusive and hence rare; (ii) identify sources of possible complementarity between the internal and external stocks of knowledge; and (iii) access and use the stock of quasi-public knowledge.

Identification and exploitation of the composition of the knowledge stock available in each (regional, technological, and sectoral) context and of the quality of the knowledge governance mechanisms play a central role in assessing the outcome of the knowledge generation process at the firm level. Some firms may benefit from a large localized stock of knowledge with a specific composition that helps the recombination process at low costs. Other firms may experience poor and expensive access to the external stock of knowledge and thus fail to generate new technological knowledge at costs below equilibrium levels.

The search for effective matching between the size and composition of localized technological knowledge stocks and the competence of each firm becomes a strong strategic imperative. Firms direct their research strategies toward intensive use of specific knowledge items that qualify the latent complementarities triggered by the composition of localized stocks of knowledge and increase the coherence between their own research agenda and the size and composition of the localized stocks of knowledge embedded in the regional, sectoral, and technological systems into which they are embedded. Alternatively, they explore other locations that provide larger levels of complementarity between internal and external stocks.

2.3 A Structured Framework

The analysis so far makes clear that decision-making in the generation of knowledge and the eventual introduction of innovations is the outcome of a multilayer and highly structured framework where different stages of analysis and causality are intertwined. In relation to the economics of innovation and knowledge, the CDM (Crépon, Duguet, and Mairesse, 1998) system of equations has become a foundation stone. The CDM approach unveils the sequential structure of the determinants and effects of the innovation process. It can be regarded as the basic framework not only for empirical and theoretical analysis of the economics of knowledge and innovation but also for an inclusive evolutionary approach that is able to grasp the complexity of economic dynamics and the analysis of knowledge and innovation as emerging system properties.

It has been the object of a variety of developments and implementations that have considerably enriched the original framework. This Element elaborates an SSE derived from the CDM approach that articulates the distinction between five levels of theoretical and empirical investigation: (i) the innovation equation where the levels of innovation effort are analyzed as the strategic outcome of a specific context of action; (ii) the knowledge generation function where innovative efforts enter as an endogenous variable next to indispensable and complementary access to the existing stocks of knowledge; (iii) the technology production function where the knowledge output accounted in the previous equation enters as an endogenous fixed variable; (iv) analysis of the selective direction of technological change; and (v) a performance equation that qualifies the effects of the costs of endogenous knowledge on productivity and profitability.

Implementation of our SSE enables us to explore the role of the creative response in the spiraling and bidirectional relationship among innovative efforts, the actual amount of technological knowledge generated and used in the downstream technology production function, and the eventual outcomes in terms of productivity-enhancing innovation that enable firms to increase their performance. It enables us to appreciate how the changing conditions of product and factor markets magnified by increasing engagement in international product markets, characterized by high levels of rivalry and substantial heterogeneity of factor markets into which competitors are based, stir the creative response on two counts: (i) they increase firms' exposure to changes in their product and factor markets brought about by the entry of new competitors; and (ii) they provide firms with the opportunity to learn from advanced competitors and benefit from relevant knowledge spillovers that are larger the closer the firms are to the international technological frontier. Consequently, it is clear that: (i) the larger firms' engagement in international product markets, the larger their likely levels of innovation effort; and (ii) the larger firms' innovation effort, the larger their competitivity in international product markets.

Levels of innovation effort are not defined in the context of standard maximization procedures where the relative costs of inputs are the exclusive determinants of decision-making. Nor are they decided by their relative costs with respect to labor, capital, and output elasticity as they do not form part of the standard substitution process between inputs that characterizes standard optimization procedures. Standard optimization procedures identify the correct levels of capital and labor under the constraint of a predetermined amount of technological knowledge that, at each point in time, can be regarded as a fixed factor.

The intentional decision to innovate and identification of the appropriate level of innovation effort are implemented in the context of the creative response. Decision-making here is determined by the extent to which the introduction of innovations is regarded as an action that is stirred by the need to cope with out-of-equilibrium conditions facing the firm and incentives to take advantage of specific market conditions, especially with respect to the conditions of access to the existing stock of knowledge. The reactivity of incumbents and entrepreneurship play a central role here.

The level of innovation effort becomes part of the knowledge generation function, which defines the amount of technological knowledge that feeds into the technology production function. Analysis of the dynamics and heterogeneity of factor markets enables us to identify the direction of technological change that can be achieved with the given amount of technological knowledge. The amount of technological knowledge and the direction of that technological knowledge form part of the technology production function and contribute to identifying the output levels. Analysis of the role of technological knowledge and the direction of technological change enables us to identify the effects in terms of productivity growth that in turn account for the dynamics of the firm's performance in terms of profitability and growth. The amount of innovation effort depends upon the extent to which the system is out of equilibrium.

In the knowledge generation function, innovation efforts are articulated through learning procedures that enable the bottom-up build-up of tacit knowledge and competence and are duly supported by efficiency wages and through formal, bottom-down R&D activities. Because of the pervasive effects of the limited exhaustibility of knowledge, the stock of technological knowledge that is internal to each firm is as much a relevant and indispensable complementary input as the stock of external technological knowledge, spilling from other firms and research activities performed in the system, that firms can access because of the twin effects of the limited appropriability and exhaustibility of knowledge.

The cost of the technological knowledge generated at each point in time is strictly contingent upon the costs of mobilizing the internal stocks of knowledge and accessing and using external stocks of knowledge. When the costs of accessing and using external technological knowledge stocks are low and the costs of knowledge as an output are below equilibrium levels, firms enjoy pecuniary knowledge externalities.

The amount of knowledge that comes into the technology production function is twice endogenous as it depends on two distinctive and relevant sequential layers: (i) the amount of innovation effort that has been selected according to the context into which the firm is embedded; and (ii) the levels of pecuniary knowledge externalities as determined by the size and composition of the stock of quasi-public knowledge available in the system and the conditions of access to it. The size, composition, and access and use conditions of the stock of technological knowledge play a central role in our approach as they determine the cost of knowledge. The lower the actual cost of external knowledge, the lower the cost of the knowledge that becomes part of the technology production function and the larger the positive effects on TFP. Firms that have access to a large stock of quasi-public knowledge and can use it at low cost in the recombinant knowledge generation function are able to generate new knowledge at costs below equilibrium and therefore can actually implement a creative response and introduce productivity-and-profitability-enhancing innovations. Firms that have no access to the stocks of quasi-public knowledge and cannot take advantage of relevant pecuniary knowledge externalities bear knowledge costs in the proximity of equilibrium levels and thus can implement only an adaptive response and introduce novelties rather than innovations. The sharper the implementation of a proper direction of technological change, the larger the effects of a creative response to out-of-equilibrium conditions will be, in terms not only of productivity but also of profitability.

In a closed economy, because of the limited appropriability of knowledge, imitators can enter the marketplace and produce the very same products at lower costs because they do not bear the costs of innovation efforts. Imitative entries drive down market prices and the profitability of innovators that can command only limited transient monopolistic rents.

In international product markets where competition takes place between firms based in capital-abundant countries and firms based in labor-abundant ones, competitors based in labor-abundant countries can imitate new products and produce them at lower costs. In the new global economy, however, firms based in industrializing countries can take advantage of the globalization of financial markets and the consequent access to financial resources with low levels of variance in global markets. Firms based in capital- abundant countries can no longer take advantage of the shield provided by the local abundance of capital.

In these circumstances, firms based in advanced countries can try to identify other key inputs that are not only locally abundant but also exclusive because they are rooted only within their own systems. Identification of rooted inputs that are characterized by high levels of resilient exclusivity plays a central role in shaping the factor intensity of the direction of the creative response. Firms able to identify inputs that can be accessed and used in local factor markets at costs that are lower than in the factor markets where competitors are based, and exploit them by systematically directing technological change toward their intensive use, may be able to increase not only TFP (at rates that are larger the lower the costs of such inputs with respect to those of other local inputs) but also the profitability stemming from the introduction of directed and biased technological change. Competitors may be able to imitate but cannot replicate the cost conditions of innovators.

This is, more and more, the case of technological knowledge: advanced countries have built a large stock of technological knowledge and have been able to elaborate sophisticated knowledge governance procedures that enable local firms to access and use it at low costs. Access to the local stock of technological knowledge and the protocols and procedures of local knowledge governance is much more difficult for firms based in industrializing countries where, on the contrary, the stock of knowledge is relatively scarce and its access cost much larger than those of the other local inputs and the knowledge costs of advanced economies. The strategic knowledge-intensive direction of technological change toward intensive use of exclusive knowledge inputs that are locally abundant but not accessible at the same conditions by rivals in international product markets can help firms to increase the appropriability of the technological knowledge generated and the innovations introduced. Rivals that cannot use the very same factor markets can imitate but cannot produce at the same costs.

The large size of the stock of technological knowledge available in advanced countries induces the knowledge-intensive direction of technological change to increase the actual levels of knowledge appropriability. This in turn yields innovative efforts that further trigger the accelerated accumulation of techno-logical knowledge and hence increase the incentive to direct technological change as a competitive tool within a Schumpeterian spiraling loop. The more resilient the knowledge cost asymmetries, the stronger the spiraling loop com-prising the selective knowledge-intensive direction of technological change, the knowledge appropriability, the rate of technological advance, and the accumu-lation of larger stocks of knowledge.

The knowledge and the human capital intensity of current technological change reflect the strategic outcome of rivalry in global product markets between firms based in advanced countries and firms based in labor markets characterized by high levels, in both relative and absolute terms, of cost of knowledge and human capital. Firms based in such labor markets have access to low-cost blue-collar labor and international financial markets that reduce capital cost asymmetries but very expensive skilled labor and access to knowledge stock. Firms based in such factor markets can take advantage of the limited appropriability of technological knowledge and imitate the knowledge-intensive technologies introduced by their rivals based in knowledge-abundant countries but cannot replicate their costs. Firms based in advanced countries, on the contrary, can take advantage of the endogenous and hence resilient supply of knowledge at low costs and increase the knowledge intensity of their production. The knowledge and skilled labor intensity of technological change enables them to increase not only productivity but also profitability and growth. The larger the cost of the basic inputs (capital and labor) in advanced countries and the larger the difference between the cost of knowledge in advanced countries and the cost of knowledge in industrializing competitors in global product markets, the larger the output elasticity of the stock of technological knowledge.

The strategic direction of technological change helps firms improve their performance on two counts: (i) matching between levels of factor intensity, determined by the output elasticity of inputs, and their relative costs helps increase levels of productivity; amd (ii) selective increase of the output elasti-city of inputs that are not only cheaper but also rare and more costly for rivals and imitators based in other factor markets helps increase the de facto appro-priability of the transient rents triggered by the introduction of innovations. The cost of knowledge is the key factor in the productivity and profitability equations, the final step of the SSE we are implementing in this Element. The performance equation establishes a direct causal relationship between the level of performance in terms of TFP and the cost of knowledge. The performance equation shows that performance will be larger the lower the cost of knowledge and the stronger the output elasticity of the technological knowledge in the technology production function.

The strategic introduction of new technologies biased toward high levels of knowledge and human capital intensity yields a Schumpeterian loop where (i) out-of-equilibrium conditions triggered by fast rates of globalization stir the creative response of firms that can take advantage of relevant pecuniary knowledge externalities, (ii) if and when a creative response is able to increase the bias toward intensive use of the quasi-public stock of knowledge that is locally abundant in advanced countries, (iii) which triggers a resilient and competitive advantage that (iv) is long-lasting because the endogenous knowledge endowment increases knowledge cost asymmetries, augmenting the levels of de facto appropriability, (v) and triggers an increase of both market shares in global markets and performance in terms of productivity, profitability, and growth. This stirs new waves of knowledge-intensive creative response that display strong path-dependent dynamics by means of which, at each point in time, past conditions exert strong effects that, however, may be changed by small events along the process.

2.4 Innovation as an Emergent System Property

The evolutionary complexity of the creative response approach enables us to understand why and how innovation is an emergent system property that takes place when the system of interactions and transactions among the agents is characterized by high levels of complementarity and convergence. A number of points are necessary to grasp this statement: let us consider them in turn.

- Economic systems are characterized by the intrinsic heterogeneity of agents. Agents differ with respect to their competence, the size and composition of their own stocks of technological knowledge, their research strategies, and their access to the stocks of quasi-public knowledge of the systems in which they are embedded.
- The price system does not convey all the relevant information: after transactions, it is interactions that matter most.
- Firms interact in both product and factor markets. Interactions in product markets enable them to absorb the knowledge spillovers of rivals. Interactions in factor markets enable them to absorb external knowledge via user–producer interactions, and in labor markets via the mobility of qualified personnel that embody relevant pieces of knowledge.

- Generation of technological knowledge is indispensable to introduction of technological innovations. Levels of innovation effort are determined by the changing evolution of product and factor markets.
- The levels of knowledge that each firm is able to generate, with their given levels of innovative effort, are determined by the size, composition, and access and use conditions of the stock of knowledge of all of the other agents in the system.
- Knowing how complementary the different pieces of internal and external knowledge are is essential to assessing the actual amount of knowledge that each firm is able to generate.
- Identifying the specific characteristics of the composition of the local knowledge stocks and actively searching for convergence of the individual research strategies of each firm are key to triggering the necessary complementarity to enhance generation of technological knowledge and hence the actual chances of making the response creative.
- Strategically directing the creative response toward intensive use of exclusive inputs that are not only locally abundant but also more expensive for competitors increases both productivity and profitability.
- The creative response stirred by out-of-equilibrium conditions in product and factor markets may trigger long-lasting Schumpeterian loops of recursive feedback that exhibit strong path-dependent dynamics.
- The Schumpeterian loop is resilient if the changes in product and factor markets and in the architecture of transactions and interactions triggered respectively by the generation of new knowledge and by the creative response at time t support new creative response at time $t + 1$. The Schumpeterian loop stops when the changes undermine the structure of interactions and transactions that favor the creative response.

Innovation is an emergent system property that takes place when agents are able to implement convergent research strategies that favor recombinant generation of new technological knowledge. Firms' strategies aimed at identifying and exploiting the latent complementarities between their own research and learning efforts and the specific characteristics of the local quasi-public stock of existing technological knowledge can lead to implementing actual coalitions for growth where each agent is able to contribute, at its own specific layer of action, in its distinctive product segment and competence, the working of actual increasing returns at the system level.

3 The Innovation Function

This section discusses what determines firms' decision to intentionally introduce innovations in response to "surprises" in their product and factor markets, such as the entry of new competitors, changes in aggregate demand, changes in consumer preferences, the introduction of innovations by competitors, and changes in input costs. Analysis of the creative response framework starts with defining the innovation function, that is, the amount of innovative effort that each firm is able to mobilize to cope with out-of-equilibrium conditions in product and factor markets.

An intentional action directed to new knowledge generation is undertaken. New technological knowledge does not fall like manna from heaven; a broad array of activities is necessary to activate the innovation process. They include not only R&D activities but also dedicated learning activities.

Also, R&D expenditures cover only a subset of the activities that are necessary in order to exploit the technological knowledge that has been generated and accumulated over time. Investment in intangible assets provides a reliable proxy for the broad array of activities that are necessary to explore the existing stock of knowledge as well as to access, retrieve, learn, absorb, and eventually reuse the knowledge that has been produced in the past, both internally and externally to the firm. Innovative efforts are indeed necessary also to absorb external knowledge (Cohen and Levinthal, 1990).

Learning provides an indispensable contribution to generating new technological knowledge. Learning is the primary source of tacit knowledge and competence. However, learning itself is not spontaneous. Efficiency wages are necessary to support and valorize the accumulation of competence and tacit knowledge by means of learning by doing, stirring the creativity of motivated workers (Stiglitz, 1974; Shapiro and Stiglitz, 1984).

At this first stage of the innovation function, firms decide how broad a range of innovation efforts to engage in, based on their firm characteristics, previous investments, and accumulated knowledge, as well as the local context. The specific circumstances of firms that are trying to meet changing product and factor market conditions play a key role at this stage.

3.1 Entrepreneurial and Managerial Characteristics

The entrepreneurial characteristics of firms play a central role. Managerial decision-making is combined with entrepreneurial capabilities in incumbents as much as in newcomers. Here, the contribution of "The creative response in economic history" is most relevant: entrepreneurs are not only the founders of – small – newcomers but also the managers of – large – incumbents. Firms differ with respect to their reactive capabilities: some firms are slower and rely less on innovative efforts as a way to cope with the changing conditions of the environment than others. Some firms are better able to take risks and cope with uncertainty than others. Here, national traditions and culture matter together with managers' selection mechanisms, their human capital levels and educational backgrounds in terms of science, technology, engineering, and mathematics (STEM), the characteristics of financial markets, and institutional, social, and economic attitudes toward – past – failure.

3.2 Performance Level

The levels of performance of firms exposed to out-of-equilibrium conditions are also important. Here, a typical U relationship between performance and innovation effort, for given levels of out-of-equilibrium conditions, is at work. Firms with above-average performance and large profits experience limited liquidity constraints. Internal funds can be mobilized and invested in innovation efforts, and their benefits in terms of equity can be appropriated without the limits of credit. Firms with high performance and large internal liquidity are likely to elaborate quickly innovative responses to out-of-equilibrium conditions of their product and factor markets. At the other extreme, firms with low levels of performance are better able to accept the high risks of innovation efforts as they have almost no alternatives. Innovation efforts are the last chance to survive. Again, these firms are likely to exhibit high levels of elasticity to out-of-equilibrium conditions. Firms close to equilibrium conditions with "normal" levels of profitability are more exposed to credit constraints and less able to face the high risks of the generation of technological knowledge and its exploitation with the introduction of innovations: they exhibit lower levels of reactivity and low levels of elasticity to the very same out-of-equilibrium conditions.

The width of the U-shaped concavity reflects the institutional context of action into which firms are embedded. Systems where tough selection mechanisms are at work are likely to have a short width of concavity: the reaction time of firms is limited and, especially, any forced exit takes place rapidly. The distribution of property rights and the active role of shareholders in the management of firms are likely to increase the width of the concavity: when shareholders retain an active role, the distribution of profits in terms of dividends is larger; the retained share available to managers to fund innovation efforts is consequently smaller (Antonelli, 2018c).

3.3 Firms' Size

The size of firms engaged in the selection of innovation efforts matters. In particular, small and medium-sized enterprises (SMEs) and young companies may encounter more difficulties investing in innovation efforts, compared to large and more established companies, due to constraints – like financial constraints and knowledge and human capital shortages – and strategic challenges – like reaching critical scale, access to complementary resources, and lack of reputation (Teece, 1986).

As far as small and young companies are concerned, the strategic choice concerning whether or not to engage in innovation activities is influenced by a number of barriers and incentives with which they are confronted due to their liabilities of newness and size (Autio, 2005; Baughn and Neupert, 2003). The main barriers to innovation efforts for SMEs and young companies are related to their primary inputs, that is, capital and labor (Söderblom et al., 2015). It is almost universally acknowledged that small firms, especially in their early stages of development, are subject to important financial constraints (Storey and Tether, 1998; Revest and Sapio, 2012). The financial literature has provided ample evidence of the existence of resource constraints and their negative effects on small and young companies' performance (e.g., Fazzari et al., 1988; Evans and Jovanovic, 1989; Holtz-Eakin et al., 1994; Blanchflower and Oswald, 1998). These financial constraints may indeed impede such firms bearing the high expenses associated with the innovative process (Hall, 2005).

Previous literature empirically confirms that the high costs associated with formal protection mechanisms are one of the main obstacles for start-ups and lead to relatively low demand for patent protection (van Pottelsberghe de la Potterie and François, 2009; Graham et al., 2010). These costs include process and translation costs, external expenses, and maintaining, monitoring, and enforcing costs (see van Pottelsberghe de la Potterie and François, 2009). Furthermore, small and young firms often lack financial resources with which to gain access to and control over the kind of complementary assets (e.g., distribution channels, brand recognition, external knowledge) that are needed to commercialize the results of their innovation activities and are thus forced to rely on cooperation with external partners, at least in their early stage of development, thus partially failing to appropriate the returns of their innovation activities.

As far as labor is concerned, the main barrier to innovation efforts faced by small and young firms concerns the rigidity of the labor market (Arvanitis, 2005; Zhou et al., 2011). This means that such firms face problems concerning how to reduce high fixed labor costs, find qualified workers, and retain them by providing the right incentives. These barriers may hamper these firms' innovative performance. In this respect, the literature on labor economics and innovation has provided evidence of positive effects that qualified personnel exert on firms' innovative performance and argued that flexibility may be particularly critical for firms in their early stage (e.g., Autio, 2005; Baughn and Neupert, 2003; Baughn et al., 2010). Flexibility of contracts allows small and young firms to use labor forces according to their available capital and thus to reduce their overall fixed labor costs (e.g., Storey et al., 2002; Zhou et al., 2011). This helps such firms to invest larger resources into innovation activities. Moreover, flexibility of contracts allows firms to improve employer–employee matching and acquire new knowledge and networks of connections embedded in new skilled employees (Kalleberg and Mardsen, 2005; Malcomson, 1997; Matusik and Hill, 1998; Martínez-Sánchez et al., 2011). Finally, flexibility of contracts can contribute to enhancing firms' innovation activities by attracting high-skilled workers, increasing workers' creative effort and participation, and easing knowledge sharing within the organization (Kruse, 1992; Collins and Smith, 2006; Liu et al., 2017; Datta et al., 2005).

As for large firms, the Schumpeterian hypothesis is masterfully summarized thus by Joel Mokyr (1990, p. 267): "large firms with considerable market power, rather than perfectly competitive firms[,] are the most powerful engine of technological progress." Schumpeter, in *Capitalism, Socialism and Democracy*, went so far as to claim that "perfect competition is not only impossible but inferior" (Schumpeter, 1942, p. 106). The Schumpeterian hypothesis has fed a long-lasting theoretical debate and the large empirical literature provides controversial evidence of the advantages of large firms over smaller ones in respect of rates of generation of technological knowledge and the eventual introduction of innovations. The results of empirical studies in different sectors, historical periods, countries, and regions have not provided conclusive evidence (Link, 1980; Link and Siegel, 2007).

Recent advances in the economics of knowledge enable us to focus the Schumpeterian hypothesis on the knowledge generation activity and on the long-lasting effects of the limited divisibility and exhaustibility of knowledge. The Schumpeterian hypothesis, in other words, would apply only to the size of the stock of knowledge and not to the sheer size of firms in terms of employment. Following this approach, Antonelli and Colombelli (2015a, 2015b) argue that the size of firms exerts negative – cost-reducing – effects when it is measured in terms of internal knowledge stock rather than in terms of sheer size. For a given size in terms of employment, firms with a larger stock of internal knowledge have lower unit knowledge costs than firms with smaller internal stocks. The advantage of incumbents, in other words, stems specifically from the effects of knowledge cumulability and non-exhaustibility and is specific to the size of their stock of knowledge.

3.4 Spillover Entrepreneurship

In a study of the knowledge spillover theory of entrepreneurship (KSTE), Colombelli (2016) investigates the relationship between the features of local economic systems, more precisely the specific influence of the characteristics of local stocks of knowledge, understood as the set of knowledge and technological competences accumulated over time in a region, and the creation of innovative start-ups. According to KSTE, new knowledge and ideas represent a main source of entrepreneurial opportunities (Acs and Armington, 2006; Audretsch et al., 2006; Acs et al., 2013).

In other words, new knowledge and ideas created in an incumbent organization, such as a firm or a university research laboratory, but left uncommercialized, may serve as a source of entrepreneurial opportunities. In fact, incumbent organizations are often unable or unwilling to fully appropriate and commercialize new knowledge and ideas generated within their research laboratories as they lack capabilities or do not want to take the risks of introducing radically new technologies onto the market; they prefer to focus on making small improvements to their existing products and processes. As a consequence, an opportunity to start a new firm is generated in order to exploit and commercialize that knowledge and those ideas. In this context, starting up a new firm is a mechanism through which knowledge spillovers from an existing organization can create opportunities for a new firm to exploit.

According to KSTE, therefore, starting up a new firm is an endogenous response to opportunities that have been generated, but not fully exploited, by incumbent organizations. As a theory, KSTE is based on Arrow's (1962b) idea that knowledge, unlike traditional production factors, is characterized by non-excludability and non-exhaustibility. This implies that knowledge is not fully appropriable and may spill over from the organization that produces it to a new organization (Griliches, 1992). An important implication of KSTE is that contexts characterized by greater amounts of knowledge generate more entrepreneurial opportunities.

The main proposition that emerges from KSTE is that "contexts rich in knowledge should generate more entrepreneurship, thus reflecting more extensive entrepreneurial opportunities. On the other hand, knowledge impoverished contexts should generate less entrepreneurship, thus reflecting fewer extensive entrepreneurial opportunities" (Audretsch and Keilbach, 2007, p. 1249).

Empirical analyses have been used to investigate and provide support to the impact of knowledge spillovers on the entrepreneurial process. However, this approach neglects that not only the size of the knowledge stock but also its nature is of some significance. Technological knowledge is not a homogenous good. In fact, a variety of competences are necessary to produce new technological knowledge. Recognizing the heterogeneous nature of knowledge means extending the KSTE proposition: not only the amount of knowledge available at the local level but also the characteristics of that knowledge have a positive impact on the formation of new firms. In this context, reconciling KSTE with the recombinant knowledge approach allows the features of the local knowledge that may affect the formation of new firms to be better qualified (Weitzman, 1998; Fleming and Sorenson, 2001). Results show, however, that local knowledge spillovers being available is not sufficient per se to lead to the creation of innovative new firms. If we look at the characteristics of the local stock of knowledge, the creation of innovative start-ups in local contexts appears to be triggered by the combination of a large variety of technologies, marked by a high degree of similarity.

Colombelli and Quatraro (2014) analyze the differential contribution of high-growth firms (HGFs) to the process of knowledge creation, drawing on the literature on Schumpeterian patterns of innovation to construct a demand-pull framework, à la Schmookler, in which sales growth is the motivation for creating new technological knowledge. The empirical results show that increasing growth rates are associated with exploration, supporting the idea that HGFs are key actors in creating new technological knowledge and showing that firms that achieve higher than average growth focus on exploration based on familiar technology. In other words, within the group of HGFs, increasing sales growth rates stimulate creation of new technological knowledge and drive search behaviors that are characterized by the screening of complementary fields across the technology landscape that are not too far removed from the firm's existing technological competences. In this respect, the distinctive knowledge dynamics of gazelles are likely to shape their positive impacts on industry dynamics (Bos and Stam, 2014).

3.5 Operationalization of the Innovation Function in the SSE Model

In our SSE model, the determinants of intentional innovative effort are captured by the innovation equation, which explores what determines firms' decision about whether to implement innovation efforts and, if so, by how much. The innovation equation frames the ingredients of the decision to innovate of each firm at time t – the levels of entrepreneurship, the U-shaped quadratic specification of performance (Π), the size of firms, and the spillover entrepreneurship – as follows:

INNOVATIVE EFFORTS$_{it}$
$$= (\text{ENTREPRENEURSHIP}_{it},\ (-\Pi + \Pi^2)_{it},\ \text{SIZE}_{it},\ \text{KSTE}_{it}). \quad (1)$$

The innovation effort of each firm at time t depends on a number of internal and external factors like entrepreneurial and managerial characteristics, performance levels, firm size, and spillover levels.

4 The Knowledge Generation Function

This section explores the knowledge generation function, the second step of the SSE model, and describes the basic ingredients and characteristics of the recombinant generation process that goes from knowledge inputs to knowledge output. The analysis summarizes, first, the role of internal innovation efforts and the internal stock of knowledge and, second, the role of the external stock of knowledge. Analysis of the cost of knowledge concludes the section.

The recombinant knowledge approach has paved the way to elaborating a new frame of analysis that is able to accommodate the central role of existing knowledge, including external knowledge, as an input into the generation of new knowledge. As Weitzman (1996, p. 209) recalls, "when research is applied, new ideas arise out of existing ideas in some kind of cumulative interactive process that intuitively has a different feel from prospecting for petroleum." This insight has led to the so-called recombinant approach: new ideas are generated by means of recombining existing ideas under the constraint of diminishing returns to scale in performing the R&D activities that are necessary to apply new ideas to economic activities. The generation of new knowledge stems from the search for and identification of elements of knowledge that have been already generated for other purposes and yet possess characteristics and properties that have not previously been considered. The search for existing knowledge items that can be recombined and used as input in the generation of new knowledge is strictly necessary: external knowledge is indispensable for the generation of new technological knowledge.

Existing knowledge is both internal to each firm, stored in the stock of competence and knowledge accumulated in the past, and external to it. In the latter case it can be accessed by means of knowledge interactions and transactions with suppliers, customers, and other agents qualified by substantial proximity. Appreciation of the generation of new technological knowledge as a recombinant process that consists of the reorganization and reconfiguration of relations among existing knowledge items enables us to better appreciate the effects of knowledge indivisibility, articulated in internal cumulability and external complementarity in the generation of new knowledge. The generation of new technological knowledge, at each point in time, by each agent, in fact is strongly influenced not only by the internal accumulation of knowledge but also by the flows and stocks of knowledge made available by the other firms that belong to the system in which each firm is embedded.

4.1 The Internal Knowledge Generation Process: Learning and R&D

Internal generation of technological knowledge, an indispensable input for the introduction of technological change, relies on two complementary mechanisms: the top-down and the bottom-up processes. Let us analyze then in turn.

The top-down process for generating new scientific knowledge consists of the creation and identification of new broad general principles and laws that are eventually transferred into the production process. The literature has dedicated a lot of attention to the top-down process and identified R&D activities as being at its core. Firms invest in basic research, implement the results with applied research activities, and finally transfer the outcome to the production side with the development of prototypes and small-scale production processes to test and implement the new technologies.

Bottom-up processes rely on learning by doing and by using. Learning processes enable firms to build up a stock of competence and tacit technological knowledge that is eventually the object of codification and generalization (Penrose, 1959; Arrow, 1962b; Stiglitz, 1987). Learning, however, is intrinsically localized as it is based on the specific techniques through which it takes place. The competence and the tacit knowledge acquired by means of learning processes have a limited scope of application that is circumscribed within a limited range of techniques measured by their capital intensity (K/L) in the proximity of those through which the learning took place (Atkinson and Stiglitz, 1969; Stiglitz, 1987; Acemoglu, 2015).

The distinction between the two processes has been used to contrast them and to identify technologies and industries where each would be more appropriate for grasping the dynamics of technological change. According to Johnson et al. (2002) and Jensen et al. (2007) there are two alternative forms of knowledge and innovation mode. The first, the Science, Technology, and Innovation (STI) mode, is based on production and use of codified scientific and technical knowledge. The second, the Doing, Using, and Interacting (DUI) mode, relies on informal processes of learning and experience-based know-how. The two modes apply to well-identified and distinct groups of firms that are active in specific industries and technologies.

Recent advances in the economics of knowledge have enabled us to blur these alternatives and highlight their intrinsic complementarity. The top-down procedure enables us to implement a certain amount of knowledge about the world (know-what), while the bottom-up procedure enables us to implement the know-how. The STI and DUI modes, in turn, are strictly complementary and implemented in parallel by the very same firms.

Both codified and tacit knowledge are as indispensable and strictly complementary in generating new technological knowledge as the bottom-up and top-down procedures are in accumulating complementary stocks of competence and scientific knowledge. In this unified context where both learning and formalized research activities are necessary and complementary, the procedures by means of which they are implemented concern the full array of industries, technologies, and firms.

Learning is stirred by efficiency wages, that is, wages that are larger than the marginal product at labor at each point in time t but match the marginal product at time $t+1$ that is possible to achieve by means of the workers' active participation and commitment. Efficiency wages are the basic tool that firms can use to stir the dynamics of the learning process and to accumulate competence and tacit knowledge. The participation of workers is as indispensable to starting the bottom-up process of knowledge generation as it is to implementing the final steps of the top-down process of applying scientific and general technological knowledge to the specific and highly idiosyncratic characteristics of the production process (Stiglitz, 1974).

Efficiency wages are the counterpart of a gift exchange between employers and employees. Employees donate their creative attention and learning capabilities, which are not part of the standard labor contract. In exchange, employers donate a wage that is in excess of the present level of marginal product (Akerloff, 1984; Akerloff and Yellen, 1986).

The excess wage should at the same time compensate the worker for their excess effort and enable them to accumulate additional competence that enables them to introduce innovations that augment the marginal product of labor. Successful innovation strategies based upon efficiency wages represent intertemporal equilibrium: extra wages paid at time t become equilibrium wages at time $t+1$. Efficiency wages are successful when firms are able to stir and capitalize on their workers' learning and then transform those workers' tacit knowledge into an input to the effective generation of new technological knowledge and the eventual introduction of new superior technologies.

An augmented learning strategy includes efficiency wages and high levels of skill and human capital intensity even beyond the requirements of the current job assignments. Learning capabilities are in fact increased by the enrollment of qualified personnel with high levels of human capital that are better able to contribute to the accumulation of tacit knowledge because of their being endowed with greater skills than are strictly required for their current tasks. Higher levels of human capital, of course, increase the gap between the current productivity of labor and its remuneration.

Combination of efficiency wages and extra-human capital identifies the broader strategy of job enrichment. The analysis of the social conditions of innovative enterprise elaborated by William Lazonick (1990, 1991, 1992, 2010), from a very different methodological perspective, stresses that the central role of learning in the organization further enriches the efficiency wages approach.

The stock of competence and experience accumulated by each firm matters as much as the flows of R&D activities and learning efforts. The internal stock of knowledge includes both the items of codified knowledge typically represented by the patents granted to each firm and the tacit knowledge accumulated by means of structured learning processes. Not only the size of the internal stock of knowledge is relevant; the composition is relevant too, in terms of both the role of codified and tacit knowledge and the different types of knowledge accumulated, in terms of technological fields of expertise.

4.2 External Knowledge in the Recombinant Generation of New Knowledge

The limited appropriability of knowledge triggers spillovers that yield external knowledge. Identification, appreciation, and accurate selection of the procedures and mechanisms that enable firms to access and use the spillover of external stocks of quasi-public knowledge become a crucial factor of strategic management. Technological knowledge in fact combines limited appropriability with limited transferability (Antonelli, 2022a).

Of course, access to and use of external knowledge are not free: relevant absorption costs are necessary to take advantage of spillovers. Already, Mansfield et al. (1981) have shown that imitation is far from free. Imitation costs are high and strongly influenced by the size and composition of the stock of knowledge available to imitators. Absorption of external knowledge requires dedicated and intentional activities. Appreciation of absorption activities and costs has two important consequences: (i) knowledge externalities reduce the cost of knowledge inputs and, as such, are pecuniary rather than technical; and (ii) the cost of external knowledge varies across firms, industries, regions, and historical time. It is far from homogenous and steady; it can be low in some circumstances and quite high in others.

Much work has been necessary to identify and explore the variety of sources of the stocks of quasi-public knowledge, on the one hand, and the variety of mechanisms and conditions that enable and qualify its access and use as an input in the recombinant generation of new technological knowledge, on the other (Antonelli, 2019b). External knowledge consists not only of horizontal spillovers but also of vertical and diagonal ones. The distinction between horizontal, vertical, and diagonal flows of knowledge spillovers is an important and recent acquisition. Spillover analysis originally focused on horizontal spillovers that flow within industries among firms that specialize in the same product range. Appreciation of other sources of external knowledge has been a major contribution of the economics of knowledge.

Relevant knowledge flows take place vertically along the user–producer interactions that complement and support transactions along value chains. Customers are sources of important knowledge for competent sellers that are able to learn from the suggestions and problems experienced by downstream users. Downstream learning by using can complement upstream learning by doing. Here, vertical Jacobs knowledge externalities play an important role and favor the growth of industrial districts away from their original mono-industrial basis. The Marshallian tradition based upon appreciation of mono-industrial districts is enriched by appreciation of the variety of suppliers and of their interactions with customers (Von Hippel, 1988, 1994, 1998).

Many seemingly unrelated activities yield important knowledge spillovers. Here, diagonal flows are at work: applications implemented in industry A can be successfully used in industry B even if no transaction flows take place between A and B. Diagonal spillover flows take place especially when general purpose technologies apply to a variety of activities (Bresnahan and Trajtenberg, 1995).

Being able to access and use the broad variety of available spillovers requires use of an array of dedicated activities. Next to imitating competitors in the same product markets, these include the broad range of activities that enable absorption of useful knowledge generated by users and customers, providers of inputs, universities, and other research centers: location in selected regions, valorization of user–producer relations, systematic interaction with universities and research centers, inclusive search for talented personnel, targeted cooperation with specialist providers of knowledge-intensive inputs, and takeover of new start-ups and small innovative firms that command useful knowledge.

Clustering of firms within a limited geographical space helps the interfirm mobility of qualified personnel and the dissemination of technological knowledge. Marshallian externalities that spill vertically across the different stages of the value chains within industrial districts help specialization in narrow technological fields. Jacobs externalities, on the contrary, play a crucial role in recombinant generation of new knowledge to positively impact the variety of firms and industries that are colocalized in proximity. In this respect, geographical closeness between firms and universities is of particular importance because the exchanged knowledge is cumulative, localized, and tacit in nature, allowing local firms to access the results of academic research more easily (Mansfield and Lee, 1996; Arundel and Geuna, 2004).

Geographical proximity is not the only thing that matters; other forms of proximity such as cognitive, organizational, and technological closeness are essential for both the learning process and the successful generation and exploitation of knowledge and capabilities (Boschma and Frenken, 2011a, 2011b; Boschma, 2005). Next to geographical proximity, technological proximity, defined as the level of overlapping of the knowledge bases of interacting partners, in fact plays a central role in reducing absorption costs and fostering pecuniary knowledge externalities (Jaffe, 1986; Colombelli et al., 2013, 2014). Technological proximity may substitute for geographical proximity: firms with high levels of technological proximity may prefer to cooperate with distant partners to reduce the risks of opportunistic behavior and better identify distinct geographical markets in which they can exploit the results of the common research.

In line with these arguments, localization strategies are relevant as geographical proximity helps with access to existing knowledge. Geographical closeness among local innovation agents (e.g., firms, universities, R&D organizations) is indeed important because the exchanged knowledge is cumulative, localized, and tacit in nature (Antonelli, 1995). Moreover, geographical proximity may strengthen other forms of proximity – for example, cognitive, organizational, and technological proximity – that are key both to the learning process and to the successful generation and exploitation of knowledge and capabilities (Boschma, 2005).

Recent investigations have explored the role of the complexity of the stock of knowledge defined as the outcome of the combination of the variety and rarity of the items that qualify a stock of knowledge (Hausmann and Hidalgo, 2009, 2013). According to the results of the empirical investigations of Antonelli et al. (2017) and Antonelli et al. (2022), complexity triggers positive effects in the recombinant generation of new technological knowledge but it can limit its exploitation in the technology production function. The complexity of the stock of knowledge augments the scope for recombination and hence the amount of knowledge that each firm is able to generate with a given budget. On the other hand, however, it has a negative impact on the exploitation of a highly heterogeneous stock of knowledge that may be larger than the positive indirect effects of the larger amount of knowledge generated upstream.

The role of universities as providers of external knowledge becomes most relevant in this context. The literature has emphasized that many factors, at different levels of analysis, may affect the effectiveness of knowledge transfer from universities to firms (Muscio and Vallanti, 2014; Bruneel et al., 2010).

At the university level, the ability of academies to transfer technological knowledge and to exert an impact on the local ecosystem is related to the institutional and organizational resources of the university. Since the upsurge of the third mission, academic institutions have increasingly faced tensions between academic excellence and research commercialization.

Previous works showed that universities need to manage this tension by acting as ambidextrous organizations (Gibson and Birkinshaw, 2004; Raisch and Birkinshaw, 2008; Tushman and O'Reilly, 1996). This is possible through creation of dual structures that provide universities with the simultaneous capability for two different but interrelated activities, that is, achieving academic rigor and commercialization. These dual structures include academic departments – the traditional academic part of the organization in charge of scientific excellence – and Technological Transfer Offices (TTOs) – separate entities within the organization that focus on the commercialization of academic research by acting as brokers between academia and industry (Ambos et al., 2008; Chang et al., 2009). Ambidexterity allows universities to combine exploration and exploitation strategies. They can explore new avenues through basic research and academic excellence while also exploiting the technological knowledge accumulated over time at the local level, through applied research that is more oriented toward the commercialization of scientific results. This exerts a positive impact on the generation of regional knowledge and innovation processes, which are affected positively by a mix of exploitation and exploration of the existing technological knowledge.

The effectiveness of academic knowledge transfer is also affected by firm-level factors. A key firm-level factor that can influence the effects of academic research on regional innovation dynamics is the absorptive capacity of local firms (Cohen and Levinthal, 1990; Fritsch and Kublina, 2018; Qian and Jung, 2017). The knowledge generation process requires a combination of diverse and complementary capabilities of heterogeneous economic actors (Nooteboom, 2000). However, given the tacit and idiosyncratic nature of knowledge, such a recombination process is not easy. Effective transfer of knowledge from one organization to another requires the recipient organization to have a high absorptive capacity for identifying, interpreting, and exploiting new knowledge (Boschma, 2005).

In this vein, Laursen et al. (2011) showed that geographical proximity increases the probability of collaboration between universities and firms. Interestingly, they also found that such a result is stronger for firms with low absorptive capacity. Unlike firms with high absorptive capacity, such firms may not have the capacity or the resources to collaborate with geographically distant universities. Firms with low absorptive capacity are thus more inclined to choose local university partners. However, the capacity of actors to absorb new knowledge also requires cognitive proximity. Organizations that share the same knowledge base are more likely to learn from each other. The effective transfer of knowledge from a university to local firms is thus affected by the degree of university–firm technological proximity (Boschma, 2005).

Finally, the effects of academic research on regional innovation dynamics are also influenced by the presence of a socioeconomic context that enables university–industry links (Braunerhjelm, 2008). Knowledge generation depends upon the ability to effectively coordinate the knowledge recombination process and the exchange of complementary knowledge among organizations within the local system. Transfer of complex knowledge thus requires close relationships between agents (Hansen, 1999; Cooke and Morgan, 1999).

In line with these arguments, Colombelli et al. (2021) developed an original framework that identifies a taxonomy composed of four models of university–region technological evolution. The taxonomy is based on two dimensions: (i) the direction of technological evolution, which allows divergent processes to be distinguished from convergent ones; and (ii) the leading role of local universities versus firms in the entry of a new technology, which allows region-pull versus university-push processes to be identified. In divergent processes, the technological specialization of universities and local firms follows different trajectories (Acosta et al., 2009), while convergent ones are characterized by increasing technological proximity over time between local firms and universities (Calderini and Scellato, 2005; Braunerhjelm, 2008). In the case of region-pull processes, local firms exert the leading role and guide the evolution of the local technological specialization (Coronado et al., 2017), while in university-push processes, regional technological trajectories are driven by local universities through their entry into new technological fields (Calderini and Scellato, 2005; Braunerhjelm, 2008).

By combining these two dimensions, the taxonomy leads to identification of four possible models of university–region that are influenced by the specificities of the local universities (university exploitation versus exploration strategies), the degree of innovation capability and absorptive capacity of the local firms (high versus low absorptive capacity), and the strength of the links between the local firms and universities (tight versus loose innovation ecosystems). The four models are:

- *convergent-region-pull processes* in which the technological proximity between firms and universities increases over time as the result of a tight local innovation system sustained by strong university–industry links (Hansen, 1999; Cooke and Morgan, 1999; Braunerhjelm, 2008). The process is mostly pulled by local firms that have high innovation capabilities and is supported by research activities conducted by local universities that leverage local knowledge and technological specializations. In this configuration, universities adopt exploitation strategies that are aimed at leveraging knowledge accumulated over time at the local level through applied research projects developed in collaboration with local firms (Ambos et al., 2008; Chang et al., 2009);

- *convergent-university-push processes* that are also characterized by tight local innovation ecosystems. However, in this case the leading role in the technological specialization process is played by local universities, which follow an exploration approach and thus contribute to the development of new knowledge and competencies in the local ecosystem (Ambos et al., 2008; Chang et al., 2009). The convergent process is made possible by the contingent high absorptive capacity of local firms;
- *divergent-university-push processes* in which the presence of universities entering into new technological fields is not enough to support a convergent process. If such universities are located in a loose innovation ecosystem, composed of firms with a low absorptive capacity, the evolution process may not lead to a convergent technological specialization process;
- *divergent-region-pull processes* that are more likely to occur in areas where local firms are characterized by high innovation capabilities and local universities adopt exploitation strategies, but their research and innovative activities are loosely related.

4.3 Kremer Complementarities in the Recombinant Generation of Knowledge

External stocks of knowledge are an essential and strictly complementary – as opposed to supplementary – input into the generation of new knowledge. At each point in time, no agent possesses all the knowledge inputs that are necessary to feed the recombinant process. Hence, agents need to access the variety of knowledge items that are possessed and used by the other firms and learning institutions that belong to the system. Both the search for and the absorption of external knowledge are necessary. External knowledge and internal R&D and learning are "Kremer" complementary.

It is important here to stress the distinction between Edgeworth and Kremer complementarity. According to Edgeworth complementarity, two activities are complementary if doing more of one activity increases the returns from doing the other (Milgrom and Roberts, 1994). Edgeworth complementarity applies to two interdependent yet separate activities, but not to the (constant returns to scale) production processes or, specifically, the knowledge generation process. In this latter case the mix of external and internal knowledge is the result of a constrained choice and includes the well-known possibility that, within the constraints of their relative costs, in order to increase output, it may be necessary to increase the amount of external knowledge and reduce the amount of internal knowledge, or the other way around. An increase of pecuniary knowledge externalities stemming from reduction of the screening and absorption costs of external knowledge leads to reorganizing the knowledge generation process with the fruitful substitution of (more) external knowledge for (less) internal knowledge, which makes it possible to increase the knowledge output. Yet none of the two inputs can be reduced to zero levels. The O-ring production process seems the most appropriate representation of the recombinant generation of technological knowledge where substitution between the basic inputs can take place but only within the well-defined limits dictated by the intrinsic complementarity of the inputs (Kremer, 1993).

In sum, new knowledge can be generated, by means of the recombination of existing knowledge items, when, where, and if:

(a) an intentional action directed toward its generation is undertaken. New technological knowledge does not fall like manna from heaven; a broad array of activities is necessary to activate the recombination process. These include R&D and learning activities, as well as other activities that are necessary to access, retrieve, learn, absorb, and eventually reuse the knowledge that has been produced in the past. This knowledge is stored in the stock of knowledge and competence that each firm has accumulated, on the one hand, and in the stock of knowledge that is external to each firm, on the other hand: this contrasts with the passive attitude that normally characterizes prospective users of technological spillovers. Learning activities are necessary in order to exploit the technological knowledge that has been generated. And while R&D expenditures cover only a subset of the broad range of innovative activities, investment in intangible assets provides a reliable proxy for the broad array of activities that are necessary to explore the existing stock of knowledge, both internal and external to each firm, in order to master the recombinant generation of new technological knowledge and exploit it;

(b) the knowledge base of each firm is identified, and the role of previous knowledge is fully appreciated. The knowledge base of a firm is identified by the size and composition of the stock of knowledge that each firm has been able to generate in the past. The knowledge base exerts its positive effects in the long run and enters the knowledge generation function directly as an input;

(c) external knowledge is a crucial, indispensable input into the generation of new technological knowledge. Because of the localized character of knowledge externalities and their strong tacit component, interactions matter. Each agent has access only to localized knowledge interactions and externalities, that is, no agent knows what every other agent in the whole system at large knows. Consequently, proximity in a multidimensional space, in terms of distance among agents and their density, matters. Agents are localized within networks of transactions and interactions that are localized subsets of the broader array of knowledge externalities, interactions, and transactions that take place in the system. The wider and easier the access to the localized pools of knowledge, the larger the amount of technological knowledge that each firm is able to generate for given levels and composition of the internal stock of knowledge and the amount of current efforts in R&D activities and learning;

(d) the stocks of external and internal knowledge and the external and internal flows of R&D activities are mutually complementary. This has two important implications: (i) no agent can generate new technological knowledge without access to external knowledge; and (ii) no agent can generate technological knowledge without appropriate internal research and learning efforts, even in a context that provides rich knowledge externalities. In other words, firms that have no access at all to external knowledge cannot actually produce any new knowledge even if they are able to mobilize large amounts of internal knowledge by means of R&D activities. Firms that have limited and expensive access to external knowledge can produce, with a given budget, a small amount of technological knowledge at higher costs. A firm that does not fund or perform any R&D activity cannot benefit from knowledge externalities and is unable to produce any new knowledge; similarly, an isolated firm localized in a context that does not provide any knowledge externality cannot produce any new knowledge.

A large amount of empirical evidence shows that strategically implementing the Kremer complementarities between bottom-up learning and top-down research activities as well as the internal and external knowledge stocks in the knowledge generation process is indispensable in the generation of new knowledge and sequentially for the growth and performance of incumbents and the creation of new firms (Antonelli, 2022b).

4.4 The Cost of Knowledge

The cost of knowledge is an important area of investigation that has so far received very little attention. Now that we have introduced the knowledge generation function, we can introduce the analysis of knowledge cost.

So far, technological knowledge has been analyzed as the output of a dedicated economic activity intentionally performed by each firm. Working along these lines, increasing evidence shows that the unit costs of knowledge differ widely across firms. Some firms are able to generate new technological knowledge with low levels of current expenditure in R&D. Others experience very high levels of current expenditure. The variance among the costs of knowledge is a fascinating area of research. Specifically, study of the knowledge cost function helps us to grasp the extent to which the cost of knowledge is affected by the availability of the full range of inputs and their costs (Antonelli and David, 2016).

As soon as it becomes evident that R&D activities are not the only input into the knowledge generation process (Gunday et al., 2011), each firm's stocks of existing internal and external knowledge acquire a new relevance as indispensable and strictly complementary inputs (Antonelli and Colombelli, 2015a, 2015b). Knowledge inputs such as the amount of external knowledge that can be accessed by firms to generate new knowledge are distributed unevenly across space. Major institutional and structural characteristics affect the actual amount of external knowledge that each firm can access and use as an input. The costs of these inputs differ in turn because of variance in the conditions of access to the available external knowledge (Cohen and Levinthal, 1990) and because of the different characteristics of the local pools of external knowledge (Saviotti, 2007; Quatraro, 2010, 2012).

By the same token, firms differ widely with respect to the size and characteristics of the stocks of internal knowledge that can be used to generate new knowledge (Jones, 1995). Knowledge inputs and outputs also vary across firms because firms differ in their specific levels of competence in managing the knowledge generation process (Nelson, 1982). Inclusion of these variables stems from identifying the recombinant character of the knowledge generation process. It enables us to appreciate the role of knowledge indivisibility, as articulated in the knowledge cumulability and the knowledge complementarity that form part of its generation (Weitzman, 1996, 1998).

Pecuniary knowledge externalities exert their powerful and positive effects by reducing the costs of upstream-generated knowledge that enters as an input into the technology production function. The final effect is reduction of the costs of the goods produced using knowledge as an input and hence an increase of productivity.

4.5 Operationalization of the Knowledge Generation Function in the SSE Model

In the knowledge generation function, the knowledge output depends on the endogenous extent of both the levels of innovative efforts identified by Equation 1 and the conditions of access to the internal and external stocks of knowledge. From this it is possible to assess the unit cost of the knowledge generated by each firm.

In this second step of our SSN, given *the levels* of innovative efforts (IE*) identified in the first step, firms try and generate the maximum amount of technological knowledge taking into account the unit costs (uc) of the broad array of innovation activities and their Kremer complementarities.

The knowledge generation function (Equation 2) identifies the key determinants of T_{it}, which is the amount of knowledge generated by each firm at each point in time, as the dependent variable of four sets of independent time-varying variables – the amount of formal R&D efforts; the efforts to mobilize learning, including the levels of wages and human capital that are in excess of the short-term labor productivity; the specific relevant characteristics of the internal knowledge base; and the amount of external knowledge. Equation 3 identifies the budget constraints:

$$T_{it} = (R\&D_{it}, LEARNING_{it}, KNOWLEDGEBASE_{it},$$
$$EXTERNALKNOWLEDGE_{it}) \qquad (2)$$

$$IE^* = (UC(R\&D), UC(LEARNING),$$
$$UC(KNOWLEDGEBASE), UC(EXTERNAL KNOWLDDGE)) \qquad (3)$$

In Equation 2 the output measure can be gauged by patents granted to each firm and by a broader set of qualitative indicators that include the number and relevance of innovations introduced.

From the knowledge generation equation it is possible to derive the knowledge cost function that identifies the key determinants of the unit cost (t_{it}) of the knowledge (T_{it}) generated by each firm at each point in time:

$$t_{it} = INNOVATIVE\ EFFORTS_{it} / T_{it}. \qquad (4)$$

Equation (4) provides a suitable specification of the knowledge cost function that accommodates, next to the role of internal learning and R&D expenditures, appreciation of the knowledge base of each firm in terms of the levels of knowledge stocks used in the generation of new knowledge, and identification of the key role of the knowledge that is external to each firm but available in regional, cognitive, and/or technological proximity. Specifically, we expect that, for given levels of endogenous innovation effort, unit knowledge costs will be lower the larger the size of the stock of internal knowledge and the larger the pool of external knowledge that firms can access as well as its consistence with the stock of internal knowledge.

5 The Technology Production Function

5.1 Theoretical Foundations

The foundation of the economics of knowledge rests on two pillars: (i) investigation of the role of knowledge in the production of all other goods implemented with the technology production function; and (ii) analysis of the activities that enable generation of new technological knowledge by means of the knowledge generation function. These two strands of the literature have grown quite apart, although both strands confirm the importance of spillovers. After seeing their significance in the technology production function, we are now looking at the role of spillovers in terms of knowledge externalities in the context of the knowledge generation function (Jaffe, 1986; Jaffe et al., 1993; Boschma, Balland, and Kogle, 2014; Rigby, 2015). The empirical evidence confirms that spillovers play a significant role in both the technology production function and the knowledge generation function (for a review of the literature, see Antonelli and Colombelli, 2015a, 2015b).

The path-breaking CDM approach has made it possible to reconcile these two strands of the literature in a single framework by means of a systemic approach where both the technology production function and the knowledge generation function are part of a single system of equations. Yet the CDM approach has not been used to investigate their sequential role for a long time. The literature provides only a few attempts to integrate analysis of knowledge externalities in the CDM approach. Ben Hassine et al. (2017) use a CDM approach, but include analysis of spillovers only in the technology production function and make no effort to account for its endogeneity.

Along similar lines, Goya et al. (2013) do not include analysis of spillovers in the "innovation equation" as they claim that "investment intensity depends much more on internal factors (such as availability of funding) than what other firms do" (p. 6). Lhuillery (2011) instead includes rivals' stock of knowledge in the R&D equation but does not take into account the role of spillovers in the technology production function. In sum, it seems possible to claim that little effort has been made, thus far, to take into account the role of knowledge spillovers in either the innovation equation or the technology production function (and productivity equations) of the CDM system. Our SSE model is thus making a step forward.

It builds upon Antonelli and Colombelli (2017), which provides an extended CDM approach through which to analyze jointly the sequential effects of knowledge spillovers in both the knowledge generation and the technology production functions. In a systemic and sequential approach, knowledge – generated in the knowledge generation function with the benefit of knowledge externalities that enable one to access and use external knowledge at costs below equilibrium – becomes an endogenous input in the downstream technology production function, where knowledge is an input next to capital and labor in the production of all other goods.

This framework enables us to confirm the strong and positive effects on the levels of output (and TFP) not only of internal knowledge but also of the external knowledge – ready to be used again – that spills from other firms that cannot fully appropriate it (Adams, 1990; Griliches, 1992). As the systematic and inclusive reviews of Hall and Mairesse (2006) and Hall et al. (2010) show, the positive effects of both internal knowledge and spillovers became one of the cornerstones of the economics of knowledge. Knowledge spilling from third parties can be used again and helps firms better to exploit their own internal stock of knowledge.

The SSE implemented by this Element allows us to grasp the sequential role of spillovers in both the upstream knowledge generation function and the downstream technology production function. The actual amount of technological knowledge that enters the technology production function is an upstream a priori that depends upon the extent to which firms try to cope with changing product and factor market conditions by means of innovation efforts geared toward changing their products, processes, organization, inputs, and markets. The actual amount of technological knowledge that firms are able to generate, once they have selected their level of innovation effort, depends upon the cost of the available external knowledge. With a given level of innovation effort, firms based in a knowledge-abundant region endowed with a large stock of technological knowledge that can be accessed at low costs and has high levels of complementarity with the firms' internal stock of knowledge and competence can benefit from large spillovers with low absorption costs and generate a large amount of new technological knowledge.

Focusing on knowledge cost enables us to identify the consequences of knowledge externalities for the upstream generation of new knowledge as an output and to assess their effects on the downstream technology production function where knowledge is an input (Antonelli and Colombelli, 2015b). The stock of knowledge that is external to each firm contributes to the recombinant generation of new technological knowledge. Because of its limited appropriability, proprietary knowledge generated at each point in time spills out of the command of the "inventors" and benefits other potential users. Inventors can retain control over their proprietary knowledge for only a limited window of time. Eventually, because of its limited exhaustibility and consequent substantial cumulability, the knowledge produced at each point in time adds to the stock of public knowledge, with a time lag due to the limited appropriation windows, so that it keeps increasing. Knowledge spillovers help to reduce the costs of external knowledge and engender pecuniary knowledge externalities when the latter enable generation of new knowledge at costs below – reproduction –

equilibrium levels. Consequently, the lower the costs of knowledge, as an output, that is generated upstream with the benefit of knowledge externalities, the lower the costs of the goods that are produced downstream using said knowledge as an input.

5.2 Operationalization of the Technology Production Function

The technology production function is a classical Cobb-Douglas production function enriched by inclusion of the stock of technological knowledge (T). In the "technology production function" introduced by Zvi Griliches (1979, 1992) the stock of technological knowledge enters as a third input:

$$Y = (K^{\alpha}L^{\beta}T^{\gamma}). \tag{5}$$

In the standard specification of the technology production function, the stock of knowledge (T) can be substituted with and by capital and labor according to the levels of the user cost of capital (r), the unit wage (w), and the cost of the technological input (t). Firms select, according to their output elasticity and relative prices, the correct amount not only of capital and labor but also of the stock of knowledge (T).

The analysis implemented so far enables firms to overcome these limitations. In our approach the technology production function is specified as follows:

$$Y = (K^{\alpha}L^{\beta}T^{*\gamma}) \tag{6}$$

where $T^* = \sum T_{it}$.

In the amended technology production function, the levels of T*, the internal stock of technological knowledge that accumulates vintages of knowledge flows that are each generated at a particular point in time, are endogenous as they are determined by the out-of-equilibrium conditions with which each firm tries to cope. In our system of equations, T* is the sum of the knowledge vintages (T_{it}) generated at each point in time (see Equations 2 and 3).

In our approach the stock of knowledge is endogenous as its generation is predetermined upstream in the sequence of equations. The amount of endogenous technological knowledge generated is determined by the innovation efforts that take place when firms respond creatively, according to the out-of-equilibrium conditions and their own specific response capabilities, and, via the knowledge generation function, depends upon the available pecuniary knowledge externalities. The endogenous stock of internal knowledge exerts a direct effect on output levels but does not substitute for and is not substituted by any other input.

The stock of technological knowledge that comes into the technology production function does not stem from a maximization process of factor substitutions. In the amended technology production function, the stock of technological knowledge neither substitutes for other inputs nor can be replaced by any other input: the existing stock of technological knowledge is the outcome of the upstream steps of much a more sophisticated decision process.

6 The Knowledge-Intensive Direction of Technological Change

6.1 Theoretical Foundations

Advanced economies are becoming knowledge economies. The structure of advanced Organisation for Economic Co-operation and Development (OECD) economies has changed drastically since the end of the twentieth century with the decline of the manufacturing industry and the emergence of the knowledge-intensive business services (KIBS) that are at the core of early twenty-first-century economic systems (Antonelli and Fassio, 2014, 2016).

The shift toward this knowledge economy consists not only in the rise of KIBS and their partial substitution for the manufacturing industry but also in the shift of the manufacturing industry, particularly of advanced countries, toward knowledge-intensive manufacture (KIM). This KIM is replacing capital intensity as the key characteristic of the production process and thus steering the direction of technological change (Antonelli and Feder, 2020, 2021a, 2021b).

Analysis of the characteristics of the knowledge generation process helps us understand the increasing role of the knowledge base as an indispensable and strategic input in the manufacturing industries of advanced countries. The evolution of the manufacturing industry of advanced economies from the last decade of the twentieth century through the first decades of the twenty-first century is puzzling. The manufacturing industry's share with respect to total employment in OECD countries exhibits a strong decline from average values in the region of 20 percent in the 1980s to 10 percent by the 2020s; its share with respect to gross national product across the same time span and the same countries has dropped much lower. The mismatch between the decline of employment and the increase of output is accounted for by increases in TFP and labor productivity.

Wage stability – and in some cases wage increase – in countries and industries exposed to the strong increase of import from industrializing countries is not consistent with expectations based upon the dynamics of factor costs equalization. The wages of importing capital-abundant countries are much larger than those of exporting labor-abundant countries and should decline toward average values that are influenced by the low levels of labor-abundant countries. The evidence suggests that factor costs equalization has not been working as expected: not only have the manufacturing industry wage levels of advanced OECD countries not been declining but they have actually been increasing.

Finally, according to evidence, the total revenue share of labor has been decreasing for the manufacturing industry as a whole at a very slow rate and with high levels of variance between and within national industries. For instance, it has been decreasing in countries like the USA and the UK, but increasing in countries such as Germany, Italy, Sweden, and Denmark and in industries such as fashion and engineering that are characterized by high levels of skill intensity and technological change that is based upon competence, accumulated by means of learning processes, and stirred by increasing wages. Within the manufacturing industry, many of the key sectors that are exhibiting a significant increase of the labor share are also characterized by faster rates of increase of labor and TFP (Antonelli and Feder, 2020, 2021b).

Of course, interpreting the strong increase of capital intensity observed in the last decade in some countries, especially in high-tech industries, should take into account the effects of the new growth accounting procedures that, since 2008, have been implementing capitalization of knowledge (Corrado et al., 2005, 2009). Capitalized knowledge as an intangible asset transforms a highly labor-intensive activity such as research into the source of a major increase in the capital figures of both national accounts and firms' financial evidence. Intangible assets now account for a large share of total capital figures in advanced countries, ranging from 20 percent in the USA and the UK to 15 percent in Germany and France.

The limited exhaustibility of knowledge fully justifies the new accounting procedures. The low depreciation rates of knowledge, however, have the "perverse" effect of transforming labor into capital with a multiplier that, following the standard 20 percent rate (Hall, 2005), fetches levels of around 3 percent. The new accounting procedures for capitalization of knowledge are inducing a strong shift in capital intensity.

When capitalization of knowledge is taken into account, it becomes evident that the increased output elasticity of capital documented by a large amount of the literature is actually determined by sharp increase of the output elasticity of intangible capital that parallels decline of the output elasticity of tangible capital. Since the end of the last century, skilled and research labor capitalized as intangible capital has become the most important production factor in advanced countries, far larger than tangible capital. Intangible capital – that now includes the wages of highly skilled labor in R&D activities – is actually replacing tangible capital (Antonelli, 2019a, 2019b; Antonelli and Pialli, in press; Antonelli et al., in press).

This combined evidence recalls the Leontief Paradox that called attention to the labor intensity of US exports in the central decades of the twentieth century. The labor intensity of exports from the USA – a capital-abundant country by definition, at that time – was at odds with the expectations of the Heckscher-Ohlin framework of analysis of international trade, according to which US exports should have been strongly capital intensive. Leontief (1953) and Baldwin (1971) provided an articulated explanation of the puzzle, stressing the role of technological change within the product cycle theory of international trade. The competitive advantage of the capital-abundant US economy was really based much more in the introduction of new products in the early stages of their life cycle than in capital intensity. In other words, US products were competitive in international markets primarily because they were new and offered an array of new functionalities that substantially increased their consumers' utility, thus replacing old and inferior products.

In the early stages of product innovation, the production process is characterized by high levels of skilled labor intensity and low levels of capital intensity. The scale of production of new products is still small and cannot yet rely on the advantages of capital-intensive mass production. The wages and levels of human capital of firms engaged in product innovation are much larger than those of firms specialized in mass production.

The evidence of the structural evolution of OECD advanced countries suggests that the Leontief Paradox is back and applies to the whole economy: firms based in advanced countries specialize in skilled-labor-intensive goods rather than capital-intensive ones as predicted by the theory of international trade. Recent advances in the economics of knowledge and innovation provide the basic tools with which to apply analysis of the Leontief Paradox to the emerging knowledge economy in OECD countries.

The starting point consists in identifying technological knowledge as the most abundant and a relatively cheaper input in the factor markets of advanced countries. The knowledge-intensive direction of technological change is appropriate for at least two complementary aspects: (i) the relative abundance of knowledge within the factor markets of advanced countries; and (ii) its relative scarcity in the factor markets of competing industrial countries.

Advanced countries are characterized by their absolute and relative abundance of technological knowledge. They command larger stocks of technological knowledge and stronger training infrastructures for generating human capital. This abundance of the technological knowledge stock has the twin effect of making technological knowledge relatively cheaper with respect not only to any other input in the local factor markets, including capital and standard labor, but also to its costs for competitors based in industrializing countries.

The large increase in the supply of human capital that advanced countries have been experiencing since the second half of the twentieth century, brought about by significant numbers of baby-boomers enrolling in universities, has contributed to reducing the relative cost of human capital. The knowledge-intensive direction of technological change in advanced countries is appropriate for two distinct and complementary reasons.

First, and most important, technological change going in a knowledge-intensive direction increases the levels of appropriability. Competitors based in industrializing countries can take advantage of unintended leaks of technological knowledge and spillovers triggered by the limited appropriability of knowledge and try to imitate, although they will need to pay higher costs to replicate the knowledge-intensive production processes of the original innovators (Antonelli and Feder, 2021a, 2021b, 2021c, 2022a).

Second, the knowledge-intensive direction increases the technological congruence of advanced countries and consequently their productivity levels. The relationship between relative factor costs and the ratio of marginal output elasticity defines technological congruence. Output levels, for a given level of total cost, are sensitive to levels of technological congruence: the larger the output elasticity of a cheaper input, the larger the output of a production function. Assuming that knowledge is the cheaper basic input in advanced countries, both the output of a production function and the output elasticity of that knowledge will increase (Antonelli, 2016).

The transition to a knowledge economy in advanced countries is faster and more effective when and where firms are able to strengthen their knowledge base and use knowledge as the prime input of the production process. Increased knowledge as the key input is based upon a mix of R&D expenditures and learning processes that are in turn based upon efficiency wages and human capital. Of course, it matters when and where the effective mix of R&D expenditures and learning takes place: the larger the wages, the larger the labor output elasticity. Efficiency wages feed the accumulation of localized technological knowledge and stir localized technological change that takes place within the technical region where learning has been taking place. The larger the output elasticity of both labor and R&D expenditures, the larger the increase of total factor and labor productivity. Increased labor output elasticity is a direct proxy of the role of the learning efforts that complement standard R&D expenditures to increase the knowledge intensity and hence, eventually, labor productivity and TFP.

Analysis of changes in the organization of global value chains and the selective division of labor within and between firms helps us to grasp an additional factor that accounts for the increasing knowledge intensity of performing firms in advanced countries. The activities retained within the boundaries of firms are more and more skill and knowledge-intensive because routine jobs assigned to low-skilled manpower at low wages, associated with capital-intensive tasks and layers of the mass production value chain, are outsourced to third parties based in industrializing countries. This process, which Katz and Autor (1999) identified as routine-biased technological change, is made possible by the adoption of information and communications technology (ICT) both on the shop floor and in clerical activities, thus enabling a core of skilled workers to control a globalized production process. These ICT-supported changes in global value chain organization affect the composition of the production process and reinforce the skilled labor and knowledge intensity, coupled with the tangible capital and the low-skilled-labor-saving bias, in the direction of technological change.

Recent advances in analysis of the classical induced technological change approach provide an additional set of powerful arguments that help us grasp the dynamics of the increasingly knowledge-intensive direction of technological change in advanced countries. According to the traditional induced technological change approach, revived by Daron Acemoglu (2002, 2003), firms direct technological change according to both changes in and levels of factor costs. According to this approach, the direction of technological change is determined by the search for intensive use of the factor that is locally most abundant and hence has the lowest cost. The relative abundance of skilled labor experienced by advanced countries since the end of the twentieth century accounts for the skilled labor intensity of technological change (Antonelli, 2016).

Analysis of competition in the global economy helps us grasp the strategic direction of technological change toward increasing appropriability levels. Competition in the global economy takes place in quasi-homogenous product markets between firms based in highly heterogeneous factor markets that rely on highly differentiated production processes and input mixes. Firms based in different countries – and regions – with different endowments and different factor markets compete in the same product markets. Factor costs equalization should drive factor costs toward convergence. Factor costs equalization, however, yields its effects with substantial delays: heterogeneity is persistent (Baldwin, 2016; Baldwin and Lopez-Gonzalez, 2015; Bloom et al., 2016).

In a static context, with a given technology and hence a given mix of output elasticities, cost heterogeneity among competitors is itself an evident source of competitive advantage: firms select the factor intensity of their standard procedures and make more intensive use of local factors that are cheaper. In a static context, cost heterogeneity is a barrier to entry and mobility with strong effects in terms of competitiveness and profitability for firms that enjoy exclusive access to factors at lower cost.

In a dynamic context, cost heterogeneity becomes a powerful factor that shapes the strategic direction of technological change. Firms that bias the introduction of new technologies toward intensive use of exclusive, yet cheap inputs – such as knowledge – that are available only in the domestic factor markets can limit the negative effects of the limited appropriability of knowledge. Competitors that cannot access the factor markets at the same conditions can take advantage of knowledge spillovers but cannot replicate the specific cost conditions of innovators. The exclusive and intensive nature of the cheap factors – such as knowledge – that competitors cannot access and use at the same conditions stretches the duration of the competitive advantage, which is less exposed to decline of appropriability and the consequent (negative) effects of imitative entry on price, market share, performance, and profits (Antonelli, 2019b).

Analysis of the strategic direction of technological change toward locally abundant and yet exclusive knowledge inputs helps us grasp the strong and increasingly knowledge-intensive direction of technological change introduced by firms based in advanced countries. Once more, the properties of knowledge both as an economic good and as the output and input of a recombinant generation process are key to grasping the role of the strategic direction of technological change toward increasing levels of knowledge intensity (Antonelli, 2018a, 2018b).

The new understanding of the strategic knowledge-intensive direction of technological change is a direct consequence of appreciating the effects of the limited exhaustibility of knowledge, which favor accumulation of a stock of quasi-public knowledge. Because of its limited exhaustibility and its consequent cumulability, knowledge is an endogenous endowment. Firms based in advanced countries have access to a large stock of technological knowledge, far larger than their rivals based in labor-abundant countries. The knowledge-intensive direction of technological change is thus both the cause and the consequence of the limited appropriability and exhaustibility of knowledge. Knowledge costs, in fact, keep declining when the upward shift of the derived demand for knowledge, triggered by the knowledge-intensive direction of technological change, is smaller than the downward shift of the supply of knowledge triggered by its accumulation. A typical Schumpeterian loop between the knowledge-intensive direction of technological change and the accumulation of increasing stocks of technological knowledge feeds the knowledge intensity of the creative response, which in turn augments the levels of de facto knowledge appropriability with increasing and persistent cost asymmetries that favor new waves of knowledge-intensive creative responses (Antonelli, 2018a, 2018b).

The resilience of knowledge cost asymmetries becomes, for firms based in advanced countries, a powerful incentive for directing technological change toward intensive use of knowledge as an input. The globalization of the economy and the sharp differences among competing countries with respect to the size, composition, and conditions of access to and use of the domestic stock of quasi-public technological knowledge have major effects on the direction of technological change. Firms based in advanced countries and engaged in international product markets have strong incentives to increase the knowledge and human-capital intensity of their production processes because they can enjoy larger pecuniary knowledge externalities and generate knowledge at costs that are far lower than those of their industrializing competitors in global product markets.

6.2 Operationalization of the Knowledge Intensity of Technological Change

The analysis implemented so far is synthesized by Equation 7, which accounts for the direction of the technological change as measured by γ, the output elasticity of technological knowledge in the technology production function (see Equation 5). The output elasticity of the stock of technological knowledge γ, which is the cheapest input in advanced countries, will be larger the larger the cost of labor (w) and the rental cost of capital (r) with respect to the cost of knowledge in advanced countries and the larger the ratio of the cost of knowledge (t) in industrializing competitors (IC) in global product markets with respect to the cost of knowledge in advanced countries (AC):

$$\gamma_{AC} = w/t_{AC}, \ r/t_{AC}, \ t_{IC.}/t_{AC}. \tag{7}$$

7 The Performance Equation

Our SSE is composed of five layers of analysis that can be summarized as follows. First, the innovation equation analyzes how firms choose whether to engage in innovation efforts by performing R&D activities and stirring learning by doing by means of efficiency wages and, if so, by how much (see Section 3). Second, the knowledge generation function explores how knowledge as an output depends on both the extent of the firm's own R&D and learning activities and the crucial role of knowledge externalities (see Section 4). Third, the technology production function explores the role of knowledge as an input next to capital and labor in the production of all other goods (see Section 5).

Fourth, analysis of the direction of technological change enables us to assess the determinants of the increasing levels of knowledge output elasticity in the technology production function (see Section 6). Finally, fifth, the performance equation, described in this section, enables us to frame the joint effects on productivity of the reduced knowledge costs triggered by the broad array of knowledge externalities explored so far (Antonelli, 2013; Antonelli and Gehringer, 2016).

This last step in the SSE is where TFP is determined by the endogenous cost of knowledge, which is the result of the estimated expenditure levels of R&D and learning activities and the knowledge output of the knowledge generation function. This specification of the performance equation enables us to account for the twin effects of the upstream knowledge externalities via the reduced costs of the knowledge generated internally. Spillovers exert their effects in Equation 3 and help to produce more knowledge. The larger the levels of pecuniary knowledge externalities, the larger, within a given budget, the expected output in terms of new knowledge and, consequently, the lower the costs of knowledge. The low costs of knowledge – reduced by the positive effects of knowledge externalities in the upstream generation of knowledge below equilibrium levels – play a positive role in accounting for the levels of productivity in downstream activities.

The introduction of productivity-enhancing innovations depends upon the extent to which firms can rely upon actual observed knowledge costs (t_O) that are below equilibrium levels (t_E). The observed cost of technological knowledge can be lower than its reproduction costs because of the pervasive effects of the limited appropriability and exhaustibility of knowledge spilling in a highly qualified context that reduces absorption costs. When $t_E > t_O$, a creative response can take place: the response becomes actually creative because it is supported by pecuniary knowledge externalities.

This is the final result of our analysis: let us assume that an economy is in equilibrium at time 0; then, changes in product and factor markets – driven by oligopolistic rivalry, changes in aggregate and product demand levels, and changes in factor markets trigger out-of-equilibrium conditions at time 1. Firms implement their responses and make new innovative efforts. When the cost of knowledge is close to its reproduction levels because relevant absorption costs limit the actual effect of potential pecuniary knowledge externalities, there is no room for any creative response: firms are able only to introduce novelties that enable them to move on the existing map of isoquants. However, when the cost of knowledge is below its reproduction levels because the positive effects of pecuniary knowledge externalities are larger than their absorption costs, firms can make innovation efforts that constitute an effective creative response:

generation of technological knowledge at costs below equilibrium levels supports the introduction of actual productivity-enhancing innovations (Antonelli and Feder, 2022b).

This leads to the final equation of the SSE model where TFP, that is, the ratio of the actual to the equilibrium output, is directly related to the ratio of the equilibrium level (t_E) of knowledge costs to the actual observed cost of technological knowledge (t_O):

$$TFP = (t_E / t_O). \tag{8}$$

When the equilibrium (reproduction) cost of knowledge is larger than the actual generation costs supported by pecuniary knowledge externalities, $t_E > t_O$ and so TFP > 1. Firms caught in out-of-equilibrium conditions in their product and factor markets can implement a successful creative response in terms of increased TFP.

The actual cost of knowledge can be regarded as an emergent property of the system into which firms are embedded. The creative response of firms is embedded in the conditions of the system on three counts: (i) the out-of-equilibrium conditions of product and factor markets; (ii) the levels of pecuniary knowledge externalities that are available at the system level; and (iii) the complementarity of the local and the internal stocks of technological knowledge.

The system is in equilibrium when the total cost of innovation effort equals its output. Innovation effort adds to output exactly its equilibrium value. In this case the actual outcome of the innovation effort is novelties, which differ from innovations. Novelties affect the characteristics of products and processes but do not increase performance and specifically do not augment TFP.

When the actual unit costs of the knowledge stock (t_O) are below equilibrium level ($t_E > t_O$), because of the pervasive effects of the limited appropriability and exhaustibility of knowledge and the complementarity of its composition with respect to the internal stock of knowledge of each firm, the output of innovation effort is larger than its equilibrium levels. The output of innovation effort is larger than its costs, too, and enables the introduction of effective productivity-enhancing innovation. In this case, firms caught in out-of-equilibrium conditions in their product and factor markets can implement a successful creative response and reap the advantages of pecuniary knowledge externalities in terms of increased TFP.

When appropriability is strong and augmented by the de facto appropriability triggered by a strategic direction that is biased toward intensive use of inputs that are not only locally cheaper but also primarily exclusive because competitors and imitators are based in different factor markets where the strategic input is rare and more expensive, firms can retain a large and resilient share of the augmented levels of TFP and profitability. When appropriability is low and firms can retain only a small fraction of the economic benefits stemming from the introduction of productivity-enhancing innovation, and the transferability of knowledge is not limited, performance is much larger at the system level than at the firm level.

The risks of Arrovian market failure are large when the transferability of knowledge is expensive because of heavy absorption costs for all but a few firms that are able to fully benefit from free spillovers. Free spillovers for a few rivals are sufficient to radically reduce appropriability and hence incentives to introduce innovations, but the system cannot benefit from the limited transferability that would provide large knowledge externalities to all firms.

8 Conclusions: Schumpeterian Loops

This Element has presented a comprehensive and inclusive evolutionary approach to economics that appreciates the complexity of the dynamics of economic systems based upon the variety of agents credited with the capability to generate technological knowledge and introduce innovations. This creative response is the outcome of interaction between firms exposed to out-of-equilibrium product and factor market conditions and the possible support provided by the system with respect to generating and using technological knowledge.

The approach has been implemented by an SSE that enables us to stress the endogenous emergence of the key variables under the control of the actual amount of knowledge externalities available in the system: endogenous levels of innovative efforts yield the generation of endogenous technological knowledge that enters the technology production function and affects, according to its costs, the actual levels of TFP and profitability.

This approach applies to analyzing the working of economic systems at large but is especially suited to understanding the dynamics of the global economy. The fast increase of globalization of economic systems has led to a new and challenging competitive context in which firms based in factor markets characterized by strong and resilient elements of heterogeneity compete in quasi-homogenous global product markets characterized by monopolistic competition. The tension between the resilient heterogeneity of factor markets and the homogeneity of international product markets is a powerful engine toward the dynamics of the creative response.

The dynamics of the creative response are shaped by Schumpeterian loops where the historic sequence of feedback is crucial to understanding their evolution. At each point in time firms try to elaborate a response to the mismatch between expected product and factor market conditions and the actual conditions.

Firms act strategically and identify the amount of innovative effort they can mobilize to introduce changes in products, processes, organization, input mixes, and markets. Their innovative efforts enable them to feed the recombinant generation of technological knowledge. Its outcome is contingent upon the size and composition of the stock of technological knowledge accumulated within the borders of the firm and the size and composition of the stock of external knowledge to which the firm has access. There being the right conditions of access to and use of the stock of quasi-public knowledge is crucial in supporting the persistence of the Schumpeterian loops.

External and internal knowledge are complementary and indispensable inputs that qualify innovation efforts. When the conditions of access to both the internal and the external knowledge stocks enable firms to benefit from relevant pecuniary knowledge externalities, the response of firms is creative. When the conditions of access to and use of the stocks of knowledge do not enable firms to generate new technological knowledge at costs that are below equilibrium because of missing knowledge externalities, the response is just adaptive and firms introduce novelties but not productivity-enhancing innovations.

The creative response, instead, enables firms to increase performance in terms of productivity, profitability, and growth rates. It enables them to increase profitability when they can direct technological change toward intensive use of exclusive inputs that are locally available at low costs but cannot be used, at the same conditions, by competitors. Being able to strategically direct technological change enables firms to contrast the negative effects on profitability of the limited appropriability of knowledge. In advanced countries that are endowed with large stocks of technological knowledge, directing technological change toward knowledge-intensive activities enables firms to counteract the aggressive competitive pressure of firms based in labor-abundant countries (Antonelli and Fassio, 2011).

Innovation efforts and their successful use in the generation of new technological knowledge have the twin effect of triggering new out-of-equilibrium conditions in global product markets that in turn trigger new responses from competitors and changing not only the size and composition of the stocks of technological knowledge but also their access and use conditions. Creation of new sources of pecuniary knowledge externalities in turn affects the chances that firms' response will be creative.

The dynamics are clearly shaped by path-dependence – as opposed to past dependent trajectories – that can yield persistent positive outcomes in terms of fast rates of introduction of technological innovations as well as decline. The dynamics of the size and composition of the stocks of knowledge as well as of the conditions of access to and use of them play a central role as engines of growth.

At each point in time, in order for a firm to flourish it is necessary for it to implement forward-looking strategies that are able to support a creative response by: (i) identifying local sources of technological knowledge; (ii) strengthening the knowledge governance mechanisms that augment the quality and viability of the knowledge interactions among economic agents and institutions; and (iii) selecting appropriate directions for technological change that augment the chances of long-lasting exploitation. Although past conditions, at both the system and the individual level, heavily affect the conduct and performance of agents, small events may improve or deteriorate the actual levels of pecuniary knowledge externalities and sustain or stop the Schumpeterian loops. When firms' responses, including generation of new technological knowledge, negatively affect the actual levels of pecuniary knowledge externalities, the Schumpeterian loops are discontinued and the system converges toward static equilibrium levels with no growth.

In the evolutionary complexity of this approach, knowledge and innovations are emergent properties of the system that may explain and support each other, contrasting the intrinsic thrusts of competitive forces toward convergence and equilibrium. They are more likely to take place when agents are able to implement effective coalitions based upon convergent research strategies that favor recombinant generation of new technological knowledge.

References

Acemoglu, D. K. (2002). Directed technological change. *Review of Economic Studies*, 69(4), 781–810.

Acemoglu, D. K. (2003). Labor- and capital-augmenting technical change. *Journal of European Economic Association*, 1(1), 1–37.

Acemoglu, D. K. (2015). Localised and biased technologies: Atkinson and Stiglitz's new view – Induced innovations and directed technological change. *Economic Journal*, 125(583), 443–463.

Acosta, M., Coronado, D., León, D., Martínez, Á. (2009). Production of university technological knowledge in European regions: Evidence from patent data. *Regional Studies*, 43(9), 1167–1181.

Acs, Z. J., Armington, C. (2006). *Entrepreneurship, Geography and American Economic Growth*. Cambridge: Cambridge University Press.

Acs, Z. J., Audretsch, D. B., Lehmann, E. E. (2013). The knowledge spillover theory of entrepreneurship. *Small Business Economics*, 41(4), 757–774.

Adams, J. D. (1990). Fundamental stocks of knowledge and productivity growth. *European Journal of Political Economy*, 98(4), 673–702.

Aghion, P., Howitt, P. W. (1997). *Endogenous Growth Theory*. Cambridge, MA: MIT Press.

Aghion, P., Jaravel, X. (2015). Knowledge spillovers, innovation and growth. *Economic Journal*, 125(583), 533–573.

Akcigit, U., Liu, Q. (2016). The role of information in innovation and competition. *Journal of the European Economic Association*, 14(4), 828–870.

Akerloff, G. A. (1984). Gift exchange and efficiency-wage theory: Four views. *American Economic Review*, 74(2), 79–83.

Akerloff, G. A., Yellen, J. Y. (eds.) (1986). *Efficiency Wages Models and the Labor Market*. Cambridge: Cambridge University Press.

Ambos, T., Mäkelä, K., Birkinshaw, J., d'Este, P. (2008). When does university research get commercialized? Creating ambidexterity in research institutions. *Journal of Management Studies*, 45(8), 1424–1447.

Antonelli, C. (1995). *The Economics of Localized Technological Change and Industrial Dynamics*. Dordrecht: Springer.

Antonelli, C. (2008). Pecuniary knowledge externalities: The convergence of directed technological change and the emergence of innovation systems. *Industrial and Corporate Change*, 17(5), 1049–1070.

Antonelli, C. (ed.) (2011). *Handbook on the Economic Complexity of Technological Change*. Cheltenham: Edward Elgar.

Antonelli, C. (2013). Knowledge governance: Pecuniary knowledge externalities and total factor productivity growth. *Economic Development Quarterly*, 27(1), 62–70.

Antonelli, C. (2016). Technological congruence and the economic complexity of technological change. *Structural Change and Economic Dynamics*, 38(C), 15–24.

Antonelli, C. (2017a). Endogenous innovation: The creative response. *Economics of Innovation and New Technology*, 26(8), 689–718.

Antonelli, C. (2017b). *Endogenous Innovation: The Economics of an Emergent System Property*. Cheltenham: Edward Elgar.

Antonelli, C. (2018a). Knowledge exhaustibility and Schumpeterian growth. *Journal of Technology Transfer*, 43(3), 779–791.

Antonelli, C. (2018b). Knowledge properties and economic policy: A new look. *Science and Public Policy*, 45(2), 151–158.

Antonelli, C. (2018c). *The Evolutionary Complexity of Endogenous Innovation: The Engines of the Creative Response*. Cheltenham: Edward Elgar.

Antonelli, C. (2019a). Knowledge as an economic good: Exhaustibility versus appropriability? *Journal of Technology Transfer*, 44(3), 647–658. https://doi.org.10.1007/s10961-018–9665–5

Antonelli, C. (2019b). *The Knowledge Growth Regime: A Schumpeterian Approach*. London: Palgrave Macmillan.

Antonelli, C. (2022a). The limited transferability of knowledge. In Audretsch, D., Link, A., Lehman, E. (eds.), *Handbook of Technology Transfer*, pp. 11–24. Cheltenham: Edward Elgar.

Antonelli, C. (ed.) (2022b). *Encyclopedia on the Economics of Knowledge and Innovation*. Cheltenham: Edward Elgar.

Antonelli, C., Colombelli, A. (2015a). External and internal knowledge in the knowledge-generation function. *Industry and Innovation*, 22(4), 273–298.

Antonelli, C., Colombelli, A. (2015b). The knowledge cost function. *International Journal of Production Economics*, 168(C), 290–302.

Antonelli, C., Colombelli, A. (2017). The locus of knowledge externalities and the cost of knowledge. *Regional Studies*, 51(8), 1151–1164.

Antonelli, C., Crespi, F., Mongeau Ospina, C., Scellato, G. (2017). Knowledge composition, Jacobs externalities and innovation performance in European regions. *Regional Studies*, 51(11), 1708–1720.

Antonelli, C., Crespi, F., Quatraro, F. (2022). Knowledge complexity and the mechanisms of knowledge generation and exploitation: The European evidence. *Research Policy*, 51(8), 104081. https://doi.org/10.1016/j.respol.2020.104081

Antonelli, C., David, P. A. (eds.) (2016). *The Economics of Knowledge and Knowledge Driven Economy*. London: Routledge.

Antonelli, C., Fassio, C. (2011). Globalization and innovation in advanced economies. In Libecap, G. (ed.), *Advances in the Study of Entrepreneurship, Innovation and Economic Growth*, vol. 22, pp. 21–46. Cambridge: Emerald.

Antonelli, C., Fassio, C. (2014). The economics of the light economy: Globalization, skill-biased technological change, and slow growth. *Technological Forecasting & Social Change*, 87(C), 89–107.

Antonelli, C., Fassio, C. (2016). Globalization and the knowledge-driven economy. *Economic Development Quarterly*, 30(1), 3–14.

Antonelli, C., Feder, C. (2020). The new direction of technological change in the global economy. *Structural Change and Economic Dynamics*, 52(C), 1–12.

Antonelli, C., Feder, C. (2021a). A long-term comparative analysis of the direction and congruence of technological change. *Socioeconomic Review*, 19(2), 583–605.

Antonelli, C., Feder, C. (2021b). Knowledge appropriability and directed technological change: The Schumpeterian creative response in global markets. *Journal of Technology Transfer*, 46(3), 686–700.

Antonelli, C., Feder, C. (2021c). Schumpeterian loops in international trade: The evidence of the OECD countries. *Journal of Evolutionary Economics*, 31(2), 799–820.

Antonelli, C., Feder, C. (2022a). Knowledge properties and the creative response in the global economy: The European evidence in the years 1990–2016. *Journal of Technology Transfer*, 47(2), 459–475.

Antonelli, C., Feder, C. (2022b). The foundations of the Schumpeterian dynamics: The European evidence. *Journal of Evolutionary Economics*. https://doi.org/10.1007/s00191-022-00794-3

Antonelli, C., Gehringer, A. (2016). The cost of knowledge and productivity growth. In Link, A. N., Antonelli, C. (eds.), *Strategic Alliances: Leveraging Economic Growth and Development*, pp. 155–174. London: Routledge.

Antonelli, C., Orsatti, G., Pialli, G. (in press). The knowledge intensive direction of technological change. *Eurasian Business Review*.

Antonelli, C., Pialli, G. (in press). Intangible assets and the productivity slow down. *International Journal of Technology Management*.

Arrow, K. J. (1962a). The economic implications of learning by doing. *Review of Economic Studies*, 29(3), 155–173.

Arrow, K. J. (1962b). Economic welfare and the allocation of resources for invention. In Nelson, R. R. (ed.), *The Rate and Direction of Inventive Activity: Economic and Social Factors*, pp. 609–625. Princeton, NJ: Princeton University Press for NBER.

Arrow, K. J. (1969). Classificatory notes on the production and transmission of technical knowledge. *American Economic Review*, 59(2), 29–35.

Arundel, A., Geuna, A. (2004). Proximity and the use of public science by innovative European firms. *Economics of Innovation and New Technology*, 13(6), 559–580.

Arvanitis, S. (2005). Modes of labour flexibility at firm level: Are there any implications for performance and innovation? Evidence for the Swiss economy. *Industrial and Corporate Change*, 14(6), 993–1016.

Atkinson, A. B., Stiglitz, J. E. (1969). A new view of technological change. *Economic Journal*, 79(315), 573–578.

Audretsch, D. B., Keilbach, M. C. (2007). The localisation of entrepreneurship capital: Evidence from Germany. *Papers in Regional Science*, 86(3), 351–365.

Audretsch, D. B., Keilbach, M. C., Lehmann, E. E. (2006). *Entrepreneurship and Economic Growth*. Oxford: Oxford University Press.

Autio, E. (2005). Global Entrepreneurship Monitor: 2005 report on high-expectation entrepreneurship. www.gemconsortium.org/file/open?fileId=47110

Baldwin, R. E. (1971). Determinants of the commodity structure of U.S. trade. *American Economic Review*, 61(1), 126–146.

Baldwin, R. (2016). *The Great Convergence Information Technology and the New Globalization*. Cambridge, MA: Harvard University Press.

Baldwin, R., Lopez-Gonzalez, J. (2015). Supply-chain trade: A portrait of global patterns and several testable hypotheses. *The World Economy*, 38(11), 1682–1721.

Balland, P.-A., Boschma, R., Crespo, J., Rigby, D. L. (2019). Smart specialization policy in the European Union: Relatedness, knowledge complexity and regional diversification. *Regional Studies*, 53(9), 1252–1268.

Baughn, C. C., Neupert, K. E. (2003). Culture and national condition facilitating entrepreneurial start-ups. *Journal of International Entrepreneurship*, 1(3), 313–330.

Baughn, C. C., Sugheir, J., Neupert, K. E. (2010). Labor flexibility and the prevalence of high-growth entrepreneurial activity. *Journal of Small Business & Entrepreneurship*, 23(1), 1–15.

Ben Hassine, H., Boudier, F., Mathieu, C. (2017). The two ways of FDI R&D spillovers: Evidence from the French manufacturing industry. *Applied Economics*, 49(25), 2395–2408.

Blanchflower, D. G., Oswald, A. J. (1998). What makes an entrepreneur? *Journal of Labor Economics*, 16(1), 26–60.

Bloom, N., Draca, M., Van Reenen, J. (2016). Trade induced technical change? The impact of Chinese imports on innovation, IT and productivity. *Review of Economic Studies*, 83(1), 87–117.

Bolton, M. K. (1993). Organizational innovation and substandard performance: When is necessity the mother of innovation? *Organization Science*, 4(1), 57–75.

Bos, J. W., Stam, E. (2014). Gazelles and industry growth: A study of young high-growth firms in the Netherlands. *Industrial and Corporate Change*, 23(1), 145–169.

Boschma, R. (2005). Proximity and innovation: A critical assessment. *Regional Studies*, 39(1), 61–74.

Boschma, R., Balland, P. A., Kogle, D. F. (2014). Relatedness and technological change in cities: The rise and fall of technological knowledge in US metropolitan areas from 1981 to 2010. *Industrial and Corporate Change*, 24(1), 223–250.

Boschma, R., Frenken, K. (2011a). Technological relatedness and regional branching. In Bathelt, H., Feldman, M. P., Kogler, D. F. (eds.), *Dynamic Geographies of Knowledge Creation and Innovation*, pp. 64–81. London: Routledge.

Boschma, R., Frenken, K. (2011b). Technological relatedness, related variety and economic geography. In Cooke P. (ed.), *Handbook of Regional Innovation and Growth*, pp. 187–197. Cheltenham: Edward Elgar.

Boschma, R., Minondo, A., Navarro, M. (2013). The emergence of new industries at the regional level in Spain: A proximity approach based on product-relatedness. *Economic Geography*, 89(1), 29–51.

Braunerhjelm, P. (2008). Specialization of regions and universities: The new versus the old. *Industry and Innovation*, 15(3), 253–275.

Bresnahan, T. F., Trajtenberg, M. (1995). General purpose technologies "engines of growth"? *Journal of Econometrics*, 65(1), 83–108.

Bruneel, J., d'Este, P., Salter, A. (2010). Investigating the factors that diminish the barriers to university–industry collaboration. *Research Policy*, 39(7), 858–868.

Calderini, M., Scellato, G. (2005). Academic research, technological specialization and the innovation performance in European regions: An empirical analysis in the wireless sector. *Industrial and Corporate Change*, 14(2), 279–305.

Chang, Y., Yang, P., Chen, M. (2009). The determinants of academic research commercial performance: Towards an organizational ambidexterity perspective. *Research Policy*, 38(6), 936–946.

Cohen, W. M., Levinthal, D. A. (1990). Absorptive capacity: A new perspective on learning and innovation. *Administrative Science Quarterly*, 35(1), 128–152.

Collins, C. J., Smith, K. G. (2006). Knowledge exchange and combination: The role of human resource practices in the performance of high-technology firms. *Academic Management Journal*, 49(3), 544–560.

Colombelli, A. (2016). The impact of local knowledge bases on the creation of innovative start-ups in Italy. *Small Business Economics*, 47(2), 383–396.

Colombelli, A., De Marco, A., Paolucci, E., Ricci, R., & Scellato, G. (2021). University technology transfer and the evolution of regional specialization: the case of Turin. *The Journal of Technology Transfer, 46*(4), 933–960.

Colombelli, A., Krafft, J., Quatraro, F. (2013). Properties of knowledge base and firm survival: Evidence from a sample of French manufacturing firms. *Technological Forecasting and Social Change*, 80(8), 1469–1483.

Colombelli, A., Krafft, J., Quatraro, F. (2014). The emergence of new technology-based sectors at the regional level: A proximity-based analysis of nanotechnology. *Research Policy*, 43(10), 1681–1696.

Colombelli A., Quatraro, F. (2014). The persistence of firms' knowledge base: A quantile approach to Italian data. *Economics of Innovation and New Technology*, 23(7), 585–610.

Cooke, P., Morgan, K. (1999). *The Associational Economy: Firms, Regions, and Innovation*. Oxford: Oxford University Press.

Coronado, D., Flores, E., Martínez, Á. (2017). The role of regional economic specialization in the production of university-owned patents. *Annals of Regional Science*, 59(2), 513–533.

Corrado, C., Hulten, C., Sichel, D. (2005). Measuring capital and technology: An expanded framework. In Corrado, C., Haltiwanger, J., Sichel, D. (eds.), *Measuring Capital in the New Economy*, pp. 11–46. Chicago, IL: University of Chicago Press.

Corrado, C., Hulten, C., Sichel, D. (2009). Intangible capital and US economic growth. *Review of Income and Wealth*, 55(3), 661–685.

Crépon, B., Duguet, E., Mairesse, J. (1998). Research and development, innovation and productivity: An econometric analysis at the firm level. *Economics of Innovation and New Technology*, 7(2), 115–158.

Datta, D. K., Guthrie, J. P., Wright, P. M. (2005). Human resource management and labor productivity: Does industry matter? *Academic Management Journal*, 48(1), 135–145.

Dosi, G., Nelson, R. R. (2010). Technological change and industrial dynamics as evolutionary processes. In Hall, B. H., Rosenberg, N. (eds.), *Handbook of the Economics of Innovation*, pp. 51–127. Amsterdam: Elsevier.

Erixon, L. (2016). Is firm renewal stimulated by negative shocks? The status of negative driving forces in Schumpeterian and Darwinian economics. *Cambridge Journal of Economics*, 40(1), 93–121.

Essletzbichler, J. (2015). Relatedness, industrial branching and technological cohesion in US metropolitan areas. *Regional Studies*, 49(5), 752–766.

Evans, D. S., Jovanovic, B. (1989). An estimated model of entrepreneurial choice under liquidity constraints. *Journal of Political Economy*, 97(4), 808–827.

Fazzari, S., Hubbard, R. G., Petersen, B. C. (1988). Financing constraints and corporate investment. *Brookings Papers in Economic Activity*, 78(2), 141–195.

Fleming, L., Sorenson, O. (2001). Technology as a complex adaptive system: Evidence from patent data. *Research Policy*, 30(7), 1019–1039.

Foster, J., Metcalfe, J. S. (2012). Economic emergence: An evolutionary economic perspective. *Journal of Economic Behavior & Organization*, 82(2–3), 420–432.

Gibson, C., Birkinshaw, J. (2004). The antecedents, consequences, and mediating role of organizational ambidexterity. *Academy of Management Journal*, 47(2), 209–226.

Goya, E., Vayá, E., Suriñach, J. (2013). Do spillovers matter? CDM model estimates for Spain using panel data. SEARCH Working Paper WP4/28. www.ub.edu/searchproject/wp-content/uploads/2013/11/WP_SEARCH-4.28.pdf

Graham, S. J. H., Merges, R., Samuelson, P., Sichelman, T. (2010). High technology entrepreneurs and the patent system: Results of the 2008 Berkeley patent survey. *Berkeley Technology Law Journal*, 24(4), 1255–1328.

Griliches, Z. (1979). Issues in assessing the contribution of research and development to productivity growth. *Bell Journal of Economics*, 10(1), 92–116.

Griliches, Z. (1992). The search for R&D spillovers. *Scandinavian Journal of Economics*, 94(Supplement), 29–47.

Gunday, G., Ulusoy, G., Kilic, K., Alpkan, L. (2011). Effects of innovation types on firm performance. *International Journal of Production Economics*, 133(2), 662–676.

Hall, B. H. (2005). Measuring the returns to R&D: The depreciation problem. *Annales d'Economie et de Statistique*, 79/80, 341–382.

Hall, B. H., Mairesse, J. (2006). Empirical studies of innovation in the knowledge driven economy. *Economics of Innovation and New Technology*, 15(4/5), 289–299.

Hall, B. H., Mairesse, J., Mohnen, P. (2010). Measuring the returns to R&D. In Hall, B. H., Rosenberg, N. (eds.), *Handbook of the Economics of Innovation*, vol. 2, pp. 1033–1082. Amsterdam: Elsevier.

Hansen, M. (1999). The search-transfer problem: The role of weak ties in sharing knowledge across organization subunits. *Administrative Science Quarterly*, 44(1), 82–111.

Hausmann, R., Hidalgo, C. A. (2009). The building block of economic complexity. *Proceedings of the National Academy of Sciences of the United States of America*, 106(26), 10570–10575.

Hausmann, R., Hidalgo, C. A. (2013). *The Atlas of Economic Complexity: Mapping Paths to Prosperity.* Cambridge, MA: MIT Press.

Holtz-Eakin, D., Joulfaian, D., Rosen, H. S. (1994). Sticking it out: Entrepreneurial survival and liquidity constraints. *Journal of Political Economy*, 102(1), 53–75.

Jacobs, J. (1969). *The Economy of Cities.* New York: Random House.

Jaffe, A. B. (1986). Technological opportunity and spillovers of R&D: Evidence from firms' patents, profits, and market value. *American Economic Review*, 76(5), 984–1001.

Jaffe, A., Trajtenberg, M., Henderson, R. (1993). Geographic localization of knowledge spillovers as evidenced by patent citations. *Quarterly Journal of Economics*, 108(3), 577–598.

Jensen, M. B., Johnson, B., Lorenz, E., Lundvall, B. A. (2007). Forms of knowledge and modes of innovation. *Research Policy*, 36(5), 680–693.

Johnson, B., Lorenz, E., Lundvall, B. A. (2002). Why all this fuss about codified and tacit knowledge? *Industrial and Corporate Change*, 11(2), 245–262.

Jones, C. (1995.) R&D based models of economic growth. *European Journal of Political Economy*, 103(4), 759–784.

Kalleberg, A., Mardsen, P. (2005). Externalizing organizational activities: Where and how U.S. establishments use employment intermediaries. *Socioeconomic Review*, 3(3), 389–415.

Katz, L. F., Autor, D. H. (1999). Changes in the wage structure and earnings inequality. In Ashenfelter, O., Card, D. E. (eds.), *Handbook of Labor Economics*, vol. 3, pp. 1463–1555. Amsterdam: Elsevier.

Kremer, M. (1993). The O-ring theory of economic development. *Quarterly Journal of Economics*, 108(3), 551–575.

Kruse, D. L. (1992). Profit sharing and productivity: Microeconomic evidence from the United States. *Economic Journal*, 102(410), 24–36.

Laursen, K., Reichstein, T., Salter, A. (2011). Exploring the effect of geographical proximity and university quality on university–industry collaboration in the United Kingdom. *Regional Studies*, 45(4), 507–523.

Lazonick, W. (1990). *Competitive Advantage on the Shop Floor.* Cambridge, MA: Harvard University Press.

Lazonick, W. (1991). *Business Organization and the Myth of Market Economy.* Cambridge: Cambridge University Press.

Lazonick, W. (1992). *Organization and Technology in Capitalist Development.* Cheltenham: Edward Elgar.

Lazonick, W. (2010). The Chandlerian corporation and the theory of innovative enterprise. *Industrial and Corporate Change*, 19(2), 317–349.

Leontief, W. (1953). Domestic production and foreign trade: The American capital position re-examined. *Proceedings of the American Philosophycal Society*, 97(4), 332–349.

Lhuillery, S. (2011). Absorptive capacity, efficiency effect and competitors spillovers. *Journal of Evolutionary Economics*, 21(4), 649–663.

Link, A. N. (1980). Firm size and efficient entrepreneurial activity: A Reformulation of the Schumpeter hypothesis. *European Journal of Political Economy*, 88(4), 771–782.

Link, A., Siegel, D. (2007). *Innovation, Entrepreneurship, and Technological Change*. Oxford: Oxford University Press.

Liu, D., Gong, Z. J., Huang, J. C. (2017). Human resource systems, employee creativity, and firm innovation: The moderating role of firm ownership. *Academic Management Journal*, 60(3), 1164–1188.

Malcomson, J. M. (1997). Contracts, hold-up, and labour markets. *Journal of Economic Literature*, 35(4), 1916–1957.

Mansfield, E., Lee, J. (1996). The modern university: Contributor to industrial innovation and recipient of industrial R&D support. *Research Policy*, 25(7), 1047–1058.

Mansfield, E., Schwartz, M., Wagner, S. (1981). Imitation costs and patents: An empirical study. *Economic Journal*, 91(364), 907–918.

Martínez-Sánchez, A., Vela-Jiménez, M. J., Pérez-Pérez, M., de-Luis-Carnicer, P. (2011). The dynamics of labour flexibility: Relationship between employment type and innovativeness. *Journal of Management Studies*, 48(4), 715–736.

Matusik, S. F., Hill, C. W. L. (1998). The utilization of contingent work, knowledge creation, and competitive advantage. *Academic Management Review*, 23(4), 680–697.

Manzaneque, M., Rojo-Ramírez, A. A., Diéguez-Soto, J., Martinez-Romero, M. J. (2020). How negative aspiration performance gaps affect innovation efficiency. *Small Business Economics*, 54(1), 209–233.

Massenot, B., Pettinicchi, Y. (2018). Can firms see into the future? Survey evidence from Germany. *Journal of Economic Behavior and Organization*, 145(C), 66–79.

Merton, R. (2013). Innovation risk. *Harvard Business Review*, 91(4), 48–56.

Milgrom, P., Roberts, J. (1994). Complementarities and systems: Understanding Japanese economic organization. *Estudios Economicos*, 9(1), 3–42.

Mokyr, J. (1990). *The Lever of Riches*. New York: Oxford University Press.

Montresor, S., Quatraro, F. (2017). Regional branching and key enabling technologies: Evidence from European patent data. *Economic Geography*, 93(4), 367–396.

Munoz, F. F., Encinar, M. I. (2014). Intentionality and the emergence of complexity: An analytical approach. *Journal of Evolutionary Economics*, 24(2), 317–334.

Muscio, A., Vallanti, G. (2014). Perceived obstacles to university–industry collaboration: Results from a qualitative survey of Italian academic departments. *Industry and Innovation*, 21(5), 410–429.

Neffke, F., Hartog, M., Boschma, R., Henning, M. (2018). Agents of structural change: The role of firms and entrepreneurs in regional diversification. *Journal Economic Geography*, 94(1), 23–48.

Nelson, R. R. (1982). The role of knowledge in R&D efficiency. *Quarterly Journal of Economics*, 97(3), 453–470.

Nelson, R. R., Winter, S. G. (1982). *An Evolutionary Theory of Economic Change*. Cambridge, MA: Belknap Press.

Nooteboom, B. (2000). *Learning and Innovation in Organizations and Economies*. Oxford: Oxford University Press.

Penrose, E. T. (1959). *The Theory of the Growth of the Firm*. Oxford: Basil Blackwell.

Quatraro, F. (2009). Diffusion of regional innovation capabilities: Evidence from Italian patent data. *Regional Studies*, 43(10), 1333–1348.

Quatraro, F. (2010). Knowledge coherence, variety and economic growth: Manufacturing evidence from Italian regions. *Research Policy*, 39(10), 1289–1302.

Quatraro, F. (2012). *The Economics of Structural Change in Knowledge*. London: Routledge.

Qian, H., Jung, H. (2017). Solving the knowledge filter puzzle: Absorptive capacity, entrepreneurship and regional development. *Small Business Economics*, 48(1), 99–114.

Raisch, S., Birkinshaw, J. (2008). Organizational ambidexterity: Antecedents, outcomes, and moderators. *Journal of Management*, 34(3), 375–409.

Revest, V., Sapio, A. (2012). Financing technology-based small firms in Europe: What do we know? *Small Business Economics*, 39, 179–205. https://doi.org/10.1007/s11187-010-9291-6

Rigby, D. L. (2015). Technological relatedness and knowledge space: Entry and exit of US cities from patent classes. *Regional Studies*, 49(11), 1922–1937.

Romer, P. M. (1990). Endogenous technological change. *Journal of Political Economy*, 98(5), S71–S102.

Romer, P. M. (1994). The origins of endogenous growth. *Journal of Economic Perspectives*, 8(1), 3–22.

Saviotti, P. P. (2007). On the dynamics of generation and utilisation of knowledge: The local character of knowledge. *Structural Change and Economic Dynamics*, 18(4), 387–408.

Schumpeter, J. A. (1928). The instability of capitalism. *Economic Journal*, 38(151), 361–386.

Schumpeter, J. A. (1911–1934). *The Theory of Economic Development*. Cambridge, MA: Harvard University Press.

Schumpeter, J. A. (1939). *Business Cycles: A Theoretical, Historical and Statistical Analysis of the Capitalist Process*. New York: McGraw-Hill.

Schumpeter, J. A. (1942). *Capitalism, Socialism and Democracy*. New York: Harper and Brothers.

Schumpeter, J. A. (1947). The creative response in economic history. *Journal of Economic History*, 7(2), 149–159.

Shapiro, C., Stiglitz, J. E. (1984). Equilibrium unemployment as a worker discipline device. *American Economic Review*, 74(3), 433–444.

Scitovsky, T. (1954). Two concepts of external economy. *Journal of Political Economy*, 62(2), 143–151.

Söderblom, A., Samuelsson, M., Wiklund, J., Sandberg, R. (2015). Inside the black box of outcome additionality: Effects of early-stage government subsidies on resource accumulation and new venture performance. *Research Policy*, 44(8), 1501–1512.

Stiglitz, J. E. (1974). Alternative theories of wage determination and unemployment in LDCs: The labor turnover model. *Quarterly Journal of Economics*, 88(2), 194–227.

Stiglitz, J. E. (1987). Learning to learn, localized learning and technological progress. In Dasgupta, P., Stoneman, P. (eds.), *Economic Policy and Industrial Performance*, pp. 125–144. Cambridge: Cambridge University Press.

Storey, J., Quintas, P., Taylor, P., Fowle, W. (2002). Flexible employment contracts and their implications for product and process innovation. *International Journal of Human Resources Management*, 13(1), 1–18.

Storey, D. J., Tether, B. S. (1998). Public policy measures to support new technology-based firms in the European Union. *Research Policy*, 26(9), 1037–1057.

Teece, D. J. (1986). Profiting from technological innovation: Implications for integration, collaboration, licensing, and public policy. *Research Policy*, 15(6), 285–305.

Tushman, M., O'Reilly, C. (1996). Ambidextrous organizations: Managing evolutionary and revolutionary change. *California Management Review*, 38(4), 8–29.

Tversky, A., Kahneman, D. (1992). Advances in prospect theory: Cumulative representation of uncertainty. *Journal of Risk and Uncertainty*, 5(4), 297–323.

Van Pottelsberghe de la Potterie, B., François, D. (2009). The cost factor in patent systems. *Journal of Industrial Competition and Trade*, 9(4), 329–355.

Von Hippel, E. (1988). *The Sources of Innovation*. Oxford: Oxford University Press.

Von Hippel, E. (1994). Sticky information and the locus of problem-solving: Implications for innovation. *Management Science*, 40(4), 429–439.

Von Hippel, E. (1998). Economics of product development by users: The impact of sticky local information. *Management Science*, 44(4), 629–644.

Weitzman, M. L. (1996). Hybridizing growth theory. *American Economic Review*, 86(2), 207–212.

Weitzman, M. L. (1998). Recombinant growth. *Quarterly Journal of Economics*, 113(2), 331–360.

Zhou, H., Dekker, R., Kleinknecht, A. (2011). Flexible labor and innovation performance: Evidence from longitudinal firm-level data. *Industrial and Corporate Change*, 20(3), 941–968.

Acknowledgments

The authors gratefully acknowledge the comments of two referees and the editor on previous versions of the manuscript, as well as the funding of the National Research Project PRIN 20177J2LS9 and the support of the local research funds of the University of Turin and Carlo Alberto College.

Cambridge Elements ≡

Business Strategy

J.-C. Spender
Kozminski University

J.-C. Spender is a research Professor, Kozminski University. He has been active in the business strategy field since 1971 and is the author or co-author of 7 books and numerous papers. His principal academic interest is in knowledge-based theories of the private sector firm, and managing them.

About the Series

Business strategy's reach is vast, and important too since wherever there is business activity there is strategizing. As a field, strategy has a long history from medieval and colonial times to today's developed and developing economies. This series offers a place for interesting and illuminating research including industry and corporate studies, strategizing in service industries, the arts, the public sector, and the new forms of Internet-based commerce. It also covers today's expanding gamut of analytic techniques.

Cambridge Elements ≡

Business Strategy

Printed in the United States
by Baker & Taylor Publisher Services